THE AI CHRONICLES

A Data Scientist's Adventures

Malaya Rout

ISBN
Paperback 979-8-89632-716-5
Hardcase 979-8-89673-446-8

This latest book from Malaya delves into various aspects of Generative AI and explains concepts relevant to different sets of people – AI specialists, Business stakeholders, General citizens and Government representatives. One thing that struck me deeply was that the author has connected various personal events in his life to Generative AI, thus establishing the fact that this technology is going to affect everyone in a very personal way.

Karthikeyan Sankaran,
CTO Exafluence Inc.

✦✦✦

This book is the perfect blend of storytelling and technical wisdom. A must-read, candid perspective making data science accessible to all.

Abhinav Kimothi,
AI leader,
VP of AI at Yarnit.app

✦✦✦

This book is an excellent resource for anyone looking to familiarise themselves with the foundational concepts of Artificial Intelligence. It offers valuable insights into the applications, limitations, and strengths of various AI processes while maintaining accessibility for readers without extensive technical expertise. It is written in easy-to-read language that anyone can pick without feeling overwhelmed.

Divya Singhal,
MBAEx (IIM Calcutta),
Batch of 2025

✦✦✦

Malaya's storytelling prowess makes this book an engaging read, while his expertise in Data Analytics ensures that the content is informative and relevant. I am confident that this book will become a valuable resource for anyone looking to make sense of our data-driven world.

Balbir Singh,
CEO,
Great Place To Work, India

✦✦✦

Narrated in an interesting story-telling style, this is a must-read book for all AI enthusiasts.

Prakash Sah,
Author and Managing Partner & Head,
Data, Analytics & AI - Manufacturing, TCS

✦✦✦

All 51 articles in Malaya Rout's "The AI Chronicles" showcase the author's passion for and expertise in AI, machine learning, and generative AI. The articles demonstrate his deep understanding of the concepts and his talent for simplifying complex ideas while connecting them to real-world scenarios. Any data science professional will appreciate the practical insights shared in these chronicles. Overall, this collection offers both depth and clarity to its readers.

TN Sreenivas,
COO Exafluence Inc.

✦✦✦

This book offers a fresh perspective on AI, exploring its practical applications through the lens of data science. Author Malaya skilfully weaves real-world scenarios into the narrative, demonstrating how data science and AI converge to solve complex business problems. With engaging storytelling and relatable characters, the book makes learning enjoyable and accessible.

Sahaya Joseph,
Vice President,
Bank Of New York (BNY)

✦✦✦

I recently had an opportunity to read "The AI Chronicles: A Data Scientist's Adventures," written by Malaya, a passionate data scientist who works as a director of data science with Exafluence. This book narrates essential concepts very smoothly - almost like chit-chat with friends. I am sure this book will be handy for data science enthusiasts.

Dr. D. Ajitha,
Associate Professor,
Department of Software Systems,
School of Computer Science and Engineering (SCOPE),
Vellore Institute of Technology, Vellore

✦✦✦

This book, "The AI Chronicles," provides a deep dive into the technical aspects of generative models, covering snippets of a data scientist's adventures. It's ideal for those with a strong technical background and a passion for solving business problems. It gives a jump start for aspiring data scientists who graduated with a Data Science Major and are about to take roles in a Data Analytics Organization.

Naina Dharmavaram,
CPO Exafluence Inc.

✦✦✦

The AI Chronicles: A Data Scientist's Adventures" by Malaya Rout is a fascinating journey through the highs and lows of data science, AI, and machine learning. Drawing from his rich experience, Rout uses relatable stories tinged with humour to walk readers through the world of data science, from a fresh grad's first job to tackling real industry challenges. The character of Siddharth brings these experiences to life, giving us an up-close look at what it's like to work with data, face the hurdles, and grow as a professional.

Rout's way of explaining complex ideas in simple terms makes even the trickiest parts of AI accessible and engaging.

What really sets this book apart is how Rout balances the technical details with reflections on the human side of AI—like ethics, culture, and how to make tech truly work for people. He dives into the promise and limitations of generative AI and makes you think about how these technologies are reshaping our world. Whether you're just getting started in data science or have been in the game for a while, "The AI Chronicles" offers valuable insights, served in a way that's easy to digest and surprisingly fun to read.

Mr Swaminathan N,
Associate Professor,
Area Head for IT & Analytics,
XIME Chennai.

FOREWORD

This book offers decluttering aspects of generative AI, delving into its underlying principles of data management, data quality, its myriad applications, and its profound implications for society. It is a testament to the incredible insights of practical knowledge condensed into chapters in a book explaining the importance of data governance, data engineering, cloud and data security as pillars for implementing perfect Gen AI capability.

As we navigate this unchartered territory, it is essential to approach generative AI with both excitement and caution. While it can be used for the greater good, the same tool can harm us if not used mindfully.

This book is a valuable resource for anyone seeking to understand the power of generative AI. Whether you are a technologist, a business leader, or simply a curious mind, you will find insights and inspiration within its pages.

Let us embrace this new intelligence era with open minds and hearts. Let us harness the power of generative AI to create a better future for all. I sincerely believe that leveraging Gen AI capabilities in different verticals with depth will be a game changer for the way businesses operate in the future.

Ravikiran Dharmavaram,
Founder & CEO,
Exafluence Inc.

FOREWORD

The book "The AI Chronicles" is an informative document that delves deep into the multifaceted world of Artificial Intelligence (AI) and Machine Learning (ML), offering insights into practical applications, challenges, and methodologies in data science. The book initiates a discussion on the balance between abstraction and explainability in AI and ML solutions. A systematic approach is presented for data preparation, including techniques such as handling missing values, outlier suppression, and ensuring variables are in their expected datatypes. Automated data visualisation techniques are discussed extensively. The book highlights the use of univariate, bivariate, and multivariate charts and stresses the importance of generating actionable insights from these visualisations. The automated training and evaluation of models are explored, with a focus on selecting high-performing models based on metrics like accuracy, F1 Score, AUC, and KS Statistic.

Furthermore, the book addresses various challenges for improving model performance. The potential and ethical considerations of using Large Language Models to create synthetic customers are examined. Guidance is provided for aspiring data scientists, including the importance of understanding the machine learning lifecycle, data exploration techniques, supervised and unsupervised learning, and temporal algorithms. There's also an emphasis on storytelling skills and managing distractions in a dynamic information landscape. The book wraps up with a reflective note on the rapid advancements in AI and ML, balancing the excitement for future possibilities with caution about the technology's limitations and ethical implications. In essence, "The AI Chronicles" serves as a comprehensive guide for data scientists, combining technical depth with practical, ethical, and philosophical insights into the evolving landscape of AI and ML. All these insights have been presented in the author's usual style, with handwritten notes for examples. Some portions have been discussed jovially, and the reader certainly enjoys this book.

Dr. V. Ramachandran,
Vice Chancellor,
Periyar Maniammai Institute of Science &
Technology,
Vallam, Thanjavur

FOREWORD

Reading the manuscript of Malaya's book reminded me of a book titled "Flight Without Formulae" by AC Kermode. 'How could a scientific and mathematical subject like flight mechanics be explained without formulae?' I wondered. I read that book for the first time, way back in 1985. But I was wrong. Often, complex subjects can be best explained with relevant metaphors and analogies without much jargon. Malaya's book on a panoramically diverse and astronomically opinionated topic - The Generative AI, once again reinforced this belief in me.

As I was told, this book is a collection of articles, mainly on the hottest topic of Generative AI, first appearing in the Times of India, written by the author himself. What amazed me was the way those articles have been organically linked, delivering a comprehensive learning experience. I loved the handwritten notes that make the effort authentic and give a feeling of guiding the reader through complex concepts of the subject. These reminded me of my school days. The celebrated subjects of AI and Generative AI have numerous advantages and applications in daily life. At the same time, let's be mindful that they can dismantle humanity if they are not kept away from the wrong hands. Hence, we must build the right kind of guardrails around the large language models. The models can be our friends or enemies. The choice is ours to make.

Damodar Padhi,
Former Chief Learning Officer of Tata
Consultancy Services,
Author of the self-help memoir 'The Scrapper's
Way: Making It Big in an Unequal World'

CONTENTS

SECTION E

THE STORM:
CHALLENGES IN GEN AI 175

THANK YOU, EXAFLUENCE

If work is worship, then the workplace is a temple. Most of the content in this book is based on the knowledge and experience gained working on the ground with the Exafluence team. Quite a few topics on data science and generative AI are picked up from deep conversations and debates at the workplace. I hope and believe the content is oriented towards thought leadership in the industry on the above two subjects.

The organisation's culture allows our laptops to become a Petri dish for growing ideas. Tolerance to and learning from failures is driven by an organisation's culture as much as by an individual's attitude towards leading life. I am good here from both aspects: organisational and individual. Being our natural self at work and in our personal life makes our whole existence stress-free. This requires us to plentifully do things we are strong in (hence, we do well and enjoy).

In addition, we must consciously and cautiously invade our territory of weaknesses and work towards overcoming them. This is a typical exploit vs. explore trade-off. No work is beneath us. Somebody who loves to code will do so even after becoming a CEO. Be biased towards action and not towards ideas. Be biased towards execution rather than towards words. This is precisely what Exafluence teaches us.

In my case, with hardly a couple more decades left in active life, there is no room for procrastination. Challenges are good. They make us stronger. At the same time, they give us opportunities for excuses. It is neither 40 hours nor 70 hours. One mantra for a good work-life balance is "If you do the things you love, people will love the things you do. Reducing the number of hours of work that you dislike does not necessarily improve your life. Work-life balance depends on what you work on instead of how long you work in a week."

I express my deep sense of gratitude to Exafluence.

NOTE TO READERS

This book is a collection of 51 articles on data science that I have published in the Times of India in one year (Nov 2023 to Nov 2024). This book adds value to the reader's experience beyond the TOI articles in the following three ways:

1) The book has a storyline and a more meaningful sequence.
2) I have thoughtfully categorised the articles.
3) I have included my handwritten notes at the end of each article. I created them by putting myself in the shoes of a first-time reader.

My biggest win is not when you buy a copy of this book. Instead, it will be when you send me your notes and claim they are better than those in the book. If you would like to give feedback or even discuss a topic on data science and Generative AI, feel free to write to rout.malaya@gmail.com

SECTION A

THE AWAKENING:
DATA SCIENCE BEST PRACTICES

Siddharth is fresh from university, landing his first job at a cutting-edge tech startup. As he dives into the exciting world of data science, Siddharth is like a sponge, absorbing knowledge and honing his skills. Each of the eleven articles in this section represents a key lesson or tool he has mastered, building his foundation in the field.

Siddharth is chit-chatting with Varun, who came over to meet the family. Varun is Siddharth's wife's colleague who is meeting Siddharth for the first time.

STRATEGY – CAN BE ABUSED
BUT CANNOT BE SKIPPED

I will tell you a joke (that has a message). I have my friend's permission to borrow. A cancer patient goes to a general physician for a check-up. The patient was as cheerful as he always was. The general physician prescribes him to meet an oncologist immediately. The patient responds with confusion, "Why are you sending me to an oncologist? The problem I must be treated for is that I am not getting worried at all about my cancer". What I want to say is "Don't solve your problem for the client. Solve the client's problem for the client".

One should first declutter the GenAI space before starting to implement GenAI-based capabilities for an organization. This holds not only for GenAI but also for the larger field of AIML (Artificial Intelligence and Machine Learning). Decluttering can be done by having an AIML strategy for the organization which should include a one-year or a two-year roadmap among multiple other things. There has to be an AIML vision that should answer the question of how the organization is going to leverage AIML to achieve its set vision. There should be a data strategy (engineering and governance), a data security strategy (sensitivity and legal), and a cloud strategy focusing on AIML. Each of the above categories should define and describe how and which technologies, processes and people need to be engaged to achieve organizational goals.

AIML programs need to be identified based on the data captured and data available. Each program ought to be assigned a priority based on the criticality of the business process it is impacting and based on the estimated quantitative business benefits it will bring to the organization. Business benefits could be revenue, NPS, profit, ranking in a forum, and so on. Quantitative business benefits should be married to the extent of implementation feasibility (another quantity) of each program. We should know how to measure the AIML value generation against each program. Revenue growth might have occurred due to a combination of factors. Our AIML solution could just be one of them. Attributing an organization's growth solely even to a diligently and meticulously implemented AIML solution is not an easy battle to win in many cases. We should also be clear on how to measure and "declare" the success of a program. There could be multiple AIML solutions under each program. Moreover, there could be multiple AIML models constituting one solution. I guess you sense the difficulty.

The next thing should be to think about how we are going to encourage, measure, and improve the adoption of AIML solutions. What is our game plan? A perfectly built solution is no solution if not adopted. We should also know what are the potential risks that the organization's AIML journey can face. And how to mitigate them. What needs to be done when one program fails, or few programs fail? Remember that I have already pointed out earlier the difficulty of defining what a failure is. Should we consider a binary success/failure outcome or an extent of success/failure outcome? A few more items that we should think about in the AIML strategy are 1) Feature store 2) Model repository 3) Deployment and MLOps process 4) Model monitoring and retraining guidelines and 5) Data quality guidelines.

One aspect that I see frequently being ignored in the industry is guidelines around how to plan for capturing additional data to enhance existing AIML solutions or to enable completely new AIML solutions. This aspect demands a foresight of at least two years or so to gather enough data points (observations) and data sets (groups of observations) for model or solution enhancements. I know, at the moment, the first objective is to make sense of how to utilize the existing data for value generation. However, it does not harm to have an idea of objective number 2. Never forget that each of the above items that I have mentioned in this article should have a corresponding Generative AI section separately to respect the intensity of impact GenAI is going to bring to each aspect of the organization.

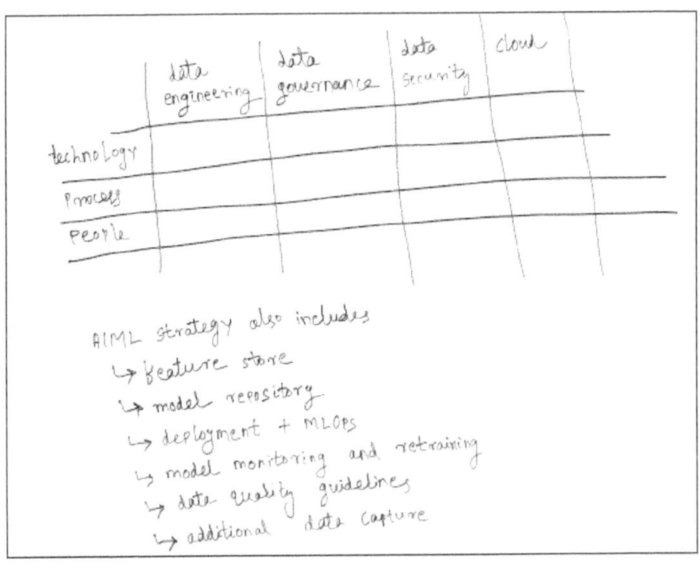

EXPLORING DATA PAINLESSLY

Building levels of abstraction simplifies and makes the interaction with a system user-friendly. An AIML (Artificial Intelligence and Machine Learning) solution with a good abstraction level will potentially have a better adoption than one not having enough abstraction. Wait a second! Where does explainability fit in? I guess we are looking at a trade-off between abstraction and explainability of an AIML solution. "I don't know what trade-off you are talking about. I would like to see the highest level of abstraction and maximum explainability". That's what an AIML user would say. I am not talking about the myriad of research on performance/explainability trade-offs being carried out currently.

To predict whether a customer will churn, we start with identifying sources (servers, databases, flat files, etc.) where relevant data for the use case is available. Then, we go to customer profile details, including demographic, tenure, and lifetime value. Customer/Organization interaction details through call centers, retail stores, and in-person sales activities are helpful. Was the organization able to close the customer's request successfully?

Was the customer left with a positive sentiment? How many service requests are pending from the customer, and for how long? Did the customer respond to the feedback survey sent across? And if he did, does he agree to recommend the organization's products and services to his friends and family? You know what I am talking about. Net Promoter Score (NPS).

Prepare the data. I mean, automate it. For example, if there are less than 20% missing values in a numeric variable, replace all missing values with the average value in the column. Replace with the most frequent value in the case of a categorical variable. If the missing values constitute a portion larger than 20%, then remove the variable altogether (just saying!). A similar customized approach can be followed for rows. Divide the variables into three categories based on domain knowledge – critical, non-critical, and good-to-have. Delete a row from the dataset if the percentage of missing values among the critical variables is greater than 75%, among non-critical is 50%, and among the good-to-have variables is greater than 25%. Have a similar suppression approach for outliers and junk values. Bring the dates into an appropriate date format. For that matter, ensure that all variables are in their expected datatypes. For example, a numeric identifier for the customer will have to be converted into a categorical variable from an integer data type. For obvious reasons, an average value of all customer identifiers does not make sense.

Explore the prepared data. Automate it. Plot a univariate chart such as a histogram for a numeric variable or a frequency bar chart for a categorical variable. Plot bivariate charts such as scatter plots (both variables are continuous), multiple boxplots (continuous/categorical), and heat maps (categorical/categorical). Similarly, we can analyse three variables together by taking color as the third variable. Analyse four variables simultaneously by taking the size of the plotted point as the fourth variable. Analyse five variables simultaneously by taking the shape of the plotted point as the fifth variable. Here is the exciting part. Generate automatic observations based on the numbers seen in the charts. In effect, it's not what is seen on the plot that will be used, but the numbers from the dataset that make the chart will be used to create the observations. From the top of my mind, "the average reduction in revenue from one region to the next is 7%" could be one such observation, assuming we have ordered the regions in decreasing order of revenue in the chart from left to right. We know that arriving at the 7% is not difficult. Moreover, with the power of LLMs (Large Language Models), we don't have a shortage of options to represent this information. If we can combine all such observations from the data exploration and extract insights that could be actionable, then nothing like it.

In addition to the above, there are pretty exciting ways of 1) Automating the model training process based on the business use case and the nature of the target variable and 2) Automating the model evaluation and selection of high-performing models. I am also thinking about a capability by which the set of model evaluation metrics is played with by the user and finalized at a desired combination of values (for example, accuracy = 90%, F1 Score = 0.84, AUC = 0.92, KS Statistic = 0.65, etc.). The tool adjusts the original dataset to the minimum extent possible to achieve that combination of evaluation metrics. Does this open up opportunities for us to take favorable business actions in a way that the variables move in the directions and to the extent they moved from the original dataset? Of course, the assumption here is that we are talking about only actionable variables. Business follows dataset instead of dataset following business. I am hinting at "expected business metrics → expected model evaluation metrics → revised dataset." Sounds hypothetical? If yes, disagree.

By enabling the data scientists to keep their hands off the data exploration, model building, and model evaluation processes, we create abstractions for them. I will discuss the automation of model training and evaluation processes in my article next week.

abstraction vs. explainability

Customer churn
↳ demographic
↳ tenure
↳ lifetime value
↳ touchpoints
↳ sentiment
↳ lending service requests
↳ NPS

data preparation
↳ missing values treatment
↳ outliers treatment
↳ cleaning
↳ datatype check
↳ aggregation

expected business metrics → Revised dataset

WHO SAID APPROXIMATION IS NOT THE KING?

"Aye mere bete sun mera kehana / Chaahe dukh hoye hasate hi rehana / Tu mere bete kyun roye / Akhiyon ke moti kyun khoye / Main tera ghoda main haathi / Main tere sukh dukh ka saathi". This is how the song from one of the Bollywood movies goes. My son grew up listening to me sing this to him. Grew up to two years and four months, I meant. He repeats the song playfully, ending with the last line, "Main tere suku kuku sa kaathi". Should I be worried about him not reciting it perfectly? Not really. This is because I love approximations. This does not mean I don't love my son more than approximations!

I cannot compel my son to either sing it correctly or not sing at all. Chances of us getting a song out of him will be very difficult. The concept of Machine Learning (ML) is based on approximation. We see the same advantages in a machine learning model. An ML model works for a wide range of unseen scenarios (scenarios that it is not trained on) only because of approximation. I could have built a system with defined rules for arriving at a decision (similar to asking my son to sing only if he sings correctly). The problem will be that the moment the inputs deviate slightly from the scope of the rules, the system does not know what to do. This sounds like a tool that predicts perfectly (100% accuracy) but only 20% of the time. The rest of the 80% of the time, it does not predict at all. What use is such a tool? Right question. There could be requirements where we might not be able to compromise on the accuracy of the recommendation. In that case, you should not build a machine learning model. You should build a rule-based system instead.

The difference between rule-based programming (traditional programming, if I can call it) and ML programming is precisely this. In rule-based programming, the inputs are given to the program to produce an output. In ML programming, inputs and outputs are given to the program (ML algorithm) to create a model. In very simplistic terms, an ML model is the "approximate relationship" between the inputs (age, educational qualification, designation, city) and the output (annual salary). The ML algorithm is able to arrive at this approximate relationship because I just provided it with thousands of examples of input/output combinations from history. Unsurprisingly, the ML model building is called "learning by examples". Once this approximated relationship is learnt, don't you think I can give you a prediction for any combination of inputs you give me? Of course, as long as I hold this relationship definition in my right hand and your inputs in my left hand, I can provide the prediction. All of a sudden, I appear like a magician. This magic is not limited to the simple salary prediction example I gave earlier. Our revolutionary Generative AI, based on LLMs (Large Language Models), works with the same principle. Instead of taking age, educational qualification, designation, and city as inputs for building the LLM, we take the first four words in a sentence as the inputs. Instead of taking the annual salary as the output, we take the fifth word of the same sentence as the output. This means that I am building a model simply to predict the next word given a sequence of words. You can easily imagine the various inputs and output (output is singular in one pair) pairs we can get from one sentence. Interestingly, in layperson's terms, LLMs are built by taking all the sentences available on the internet. I guess you get a sense of the volume of inputs-output examples we provided to our LLM for learning. Won't the LLM create magic with such "knowledge"?

rule based vs. approximation based

predictions have inaccuracies

model is approximate relationship between inputs and output

LLM is an ML model

rule based vs. approximation based

predictions have inaccuracies

model is approximate relationship between inputs and output

LLM is an ML model

THAT MODELLING
ALGORITHM ON THE CV

L ife is a break between two deaths. Building a machine learning model is a break from data exploration. I am not implying that data exploration is scary, like death, while model building is complete with life. I am just saying that we have spent more time dead than alive. Technical prowess is essential to being a good data scientist. Domain knowledge and story-telling are also crucial. Technical skills encapsulate expertise in statistical concepts, programming, visualisation, and machine learning. Nowadays, a good data scientist knows Generative AI apart from everything else.

A model that does not solve a business problem well but is used frequently to comply with the pressure of adopting analytics is like a cancer to business. On the other hand, a model that recommends well but is not used enough by users due to a lack of sensitisation to the benefits of analytics is a loss of opportunity. Either way, data does not play the pivotal role it should play in giving a competitive advantage to the organisation. Data science is not machine learning (training the model) alone. It includes all activities from understanding the business problem to finally implementing and monitoring the solution in the production environment. The outcome of this exercise should be an end-to-end solution that should flourish in tandem with other existing IT applications.

Attributing revenue growth to an analytics solution alone is very tricky. One must be careful to eliminate all other possible revenue boosters in that case. Converting a business problem statement to an analytics problem statement is equally tricky. For example, let us say that the business problem is that the organisation's revenue has decreased consistently over the last four years. For the moment, assume the scope of the problem statement, such as which products are hit, over what timeline, and to what extent of decline.

What could be the various possible analytics statements? 1) Identify high-potential products that the sales team can focus on, 2) Identify high-potential prospects that the marketing team could target with their customised and personalised campaigns, 3) How much to spend on which channel for best returns, 4) Forecast subsequent quarter sales and alert with recommendations, and

5) Predict ticket resolution time and use that for proactive communication to improve customer experience. The above options need to be discussed with business stakeholders. One or more of them should be selected to build a solution on. Each option above has a unique way of increasing revenue. We must quantify the impact of each of the five solutions on revenue and then pick up the top two or three solutions by discussing them with the business teams. Remember that all five solutions need not cater to the same business team, which means five different teams can come forward simultaneously and show an interest. The first solution might interest the sales team. The second and third ones could be for the marketing team. The fourth one will benefit the supply chain team. The fifth one will relate to the service assurance team. Ranking the solutions with respect to their impact on the overall business and ease of implementation will help prioritise.

Training a model is not a mandatory activity in a data science project. You will often encounter situations where an exploratory data analysis (EDA) alone can provide the necessary insights. When the business team uses the insight to solve their problem, it becomes an elegant analytics solution. One must keep this in mind even though we love to see the long list of modelling algorithms on the CV. If you have already decided to lose the algorithm and include the solution on your CV by now, I will not mind.

Solving business Problem Vs. building models

adoption leads to success

data exploration > building models

one business Problem → analytics problem 1
→ analytics Problem 2
→ analytics Problem 3

HAIRCUT NOT THE ONLY WAY TO DECLUTTER YOUR HEAD

An individual learns best through a specific way of communication. Some prefer writing, some listen, and others read. In my case, writing leads to more learning than listening or reading. I remember the crazy long notes we produced as school-going children by the end of every class. At times, the focus would be more on the speed of scribbling everything the teacher uttered than learning. Imagine somebody's class notes having "hmm uhm aachhoon". The sincere most disciple, I would say! Immediately after the scribbling wars, we would count and compare the number of pages we wrote with those of friends. I have very knowledgeable friends who have ditched note-taking during school days. I didn't know there was an option! I didn't know there was a different way of learning than taking notes. You are right. I come from a background where exams were more of a test of memory than that of learning! By the way, I had jotted down the skeleton of this article using my phone while we waited at the bank for our turn. Note-taking these days!

I have been frequently using mind maps lately. I find that a helpful way of note-taking. A mind map gives a holistic view of a topic. It helps organise my chaotic thoughts in a structured way. The less I talk about what goes on inside my head, the better it is. There are plenty of online tools available to draw mind maps. It being digital gives us certain advantages. We can hide and show branches, making it possible to view the level we desire to see. There is practically no limit to how deep we can go. You can convey the lay of the land effectively. Not only that, but it also works as a handy tool for future reference. The closest structure we have to a mind map is a table of contents in a book.

If a candidate can draw a mind map using pen and paper during an interview, there is a high chance that they understand the topic well. To create one, you need expertise on the subject. If I am unsure whether a specific piece of content goes on one branch or another, I have problems with that subject. These days, I am trying to follow a practice. Whenever I go through something or learn something new, I create a mind map and share it with the team. It becomes a living document as we can return and add more branches when we learn more about the topic. While I am sure such tools have many more capabilities, I use the basic ones. I try to keep it limited to only the node's name. You can usually add images and additional text to each node. Please don't take the simplicity away from me!

I cannot close an article without talking about AI. Guess what! The tool also allows for AI-generated mind maps. You give a topic, and you get a bunch of branches and sub-branches generated within seconds. While I appreciate the "mind-mapic" leap into the future, AI-generated maps were not impressive. An AI-generated mind map with AI as the topic was not remarkable either. I guess AI is not a good auto-biographer.

ML is a subset of AI, DL is a subset of ML, and LLM is a subset of DL. AI is the creation of intelligent agents. Contrast it with natural intelligence. ML is the exercise of training models, evaluating them and using the best one to predict. Deep learning models learn more complex patterns than regular ML can do. LLMs are generative pre-trained language models that evolved from a specific type of DL. It was much easier to understand when I represented this information (and plenty more) in the form of a mind map titled "Data Science Fundamentals", having 293 branches. A different mind map, "Large Language Models", came up to 291 branches.

UFF! THE ILLUSION THAT AI IS

Workplaces (even the virtual ones) are good places to flex your brain muscles. The following content results from yesterday's conversation with my colleague. Saturday morning laziness has made me pick up a few of his texts without modification.

Generative AI is built on the back of large language models (LLMs). This revolutionary technology has countless applications in document processing, synthetic data generation, data exploration, language translation, summarisation, writing poems and stories, editing tasks, code generation, chatbots, and enhancing customer experience. The list of use cases is limited only by our imagination. No industry and no business function are untouched. After all, this is only a creative speck of the human mind. Those who believe AI will replace human intelligence, please talk to the ones who don't think so. If I am asked, you will get human intelligence: no, human writing: (open-mouthed stare at the 27-inch monitor with the usual lack of handsomeness)!

LLMs generate text by predicting the next word given the context of the previous sequence of words. The closeness of context is determined numerically by converting words into vectors, which are numerical representations of words. That is the extent to which LLMs understand a language. While I hesitate to state that they 'understand' human languages, this is definitely a step forward towards machines mimicking human intelligence. They predict the next word so accurately that it gives the illusion of language understanding. Keep in mind that LLM is not an alternative to Google search. Google search picks from existing content and displays them as results. LLMs actually generate new content. No searching happens.

Similarly, ML models give the illusion of understanding the real world. An ML model can predict the correct output even though it has no clue about the underlying data-generation process. During the model-building process, the model performances are evaluated based on outcomes as available in the training dataset. The problem in finalising the model based on outcomes without understanding the underlying mechanics is that any change in the real world causes some changes to the input. This, in turn, can potentially result in significant changes to outcomes. The finalised model would go out of track completely. Therefore, we see models drifting over time.

LLMs give us the illusion of understanding the language better. They are more stable when differing inputs are used than classical ML models. Classical ML models work on data (mostly numbers), while LLMs work on languages. This comparison between data and language is interesting. Languages are more informative and expressive than numbers. That's the reason we ultimately prefer to narrate the story hidden in numbers using a language.

The invincible-looking LLMs will fail the moment English grammar rules change, causing modifications in our way of writing (hypothetically). English is just an example. Recreating the training dataset for LLMs will require a few more decades of creating new online content.

It is not too far-fetched to say we are heading towards such a scenario. Relax, grammar rules are not changing! However, we are creating a lot of online text using Generative AI tools. LLMs generate "human-like" text. Only humans can generate human text. When the LLMs need to be re-trained on newer textual data ten years from now, seventy per cent (guessing the number) of the text will be human-like text. Therefore, in the form of LLM outputs, we will soon be reading something which is like human-like. As I always say, nobody has ever experienced the future. The moment the future arrives, it transforms itself into the present. So, let's wait and see what the "present" holds for us. Only time will tell.

IT IS A TOPATO

The daycare teacher asks, "What is this?" My son replies, "Tomato." She says, "Good. What is this?" My son answers, "Topato." She clarifies, "It is called Potato." My son exclaims, "Aan?" with a puzzled look. My wife and I hereby admit on the record that we taught our son it was a Topato. It cannot be construed as an admission applicable to all the mistakes he will make in the future. There were three reasons for doing so. 1) Our curiosity to find out how long it takes for a kid to discover the truth. 2) He must be taught that parents can be wrong. 3) Fun.

My son encountered something I call a teacher-parent trade-off. This condenses to TOPATO. I know TO does not exactly expand to TEACHER. However, it fits well with the story. During our early school days, a teacher's decision was the final decision in answering questions such as 'How many teeth did a human being have'? Thanks to the subjectivity in interpreting the question. During the growing-up process, at some point, parents started making more sense than teachers with their answers. And by the time we cross 40, neither teachers nor parents make sense anymore.

After all, we have more achievements than those combined in both! What were they doing if not posting online?

If you are wondering, I will link it to data science. I was browsing to understand the difference between a T-shaped and a V-shaped skill set. The search results confused me. It seemed like the Internet was wrong. It is almost like saying parents or teachers could be wrong, leading to the abovementioned trade-off. Got the connection now?

I will tell you about the tectonic shift in talent expectations in the AIML industry. Ten years ago, it was enough if you knew only one tool (for example, Tableau), only one programming language (let us say R), or only one database (Oracle). It was enough to be a deep expert in one skill and have surface-level expertise in many other skills (avoiding using 'superficial' as it sounds so negative). This is what I guess I can call a T-shaped skill set.

Today, it is not enough. I cannot say that I am an ML expert, and my only job is to train models, evaluate them, and finalise the best one. By doing that, I am leaving the data collection, data preparation, model deployment, model integration with the business process, model inferencing and the plethora of decisions to other people and teams. For that matter, I must know how to collaborate and provide inputs on the work happening to my left and right while delivering a solution to a business problem. As a data scientist, do I expect someone else to create the slides (saying I am not good with the choice of colours) and a third person to do the talking (saying I am not good at explaining) to present the solution to the business team? I need to be a deep expert in one area. I can be less deep in the two work areas surrounding me, further less deep in work areas surrounding those two and so on. That is what I call a V-shaped skill set. As a data scientist, can I write the script to move the data from a source to the target database? Should I not be aware of which data privacy regulations apply to the country the data originates from? Which fields are sensitive? Which customer's records need to be removed before I get my hands on the data? Of course, that impacts the behaviour of the ML model I will build and deliver. This overlap of roles is evident in smaller teams, which are five or six-human armies. Talk about my using gender-sensitive language!

Extrapolating on the above thought, we probably now see the need for comb-shaped skill sets. A data scientist might not only need to "collaborate" and "help" a data engineer in consolidating and moving the data but must do it himself. Hence, there is a need for deep expertise in multiple facets, such as AIML theoretical concepts, technologies, tools, programming languages, databases, user interfaces, and communication (listening, writing, and speaking). Therefore, if you are an ML model-building expert, do not be surprised if your manager calls and asks you to fix issues with MLOps (Machine Learning Operations).

TOPATO nearly stands for
Teacher - parent trade off

T shaped vs. V shaped skillset

need of the hour is
V shaped learning

expectations of industry
from AIML candidates

THE MULTIPLE WORLDS OF MINE

"**P**apa, look. The white train is sitting on the blue car". First, I have never noticed the colour of things as much. He has the habit of qualifying everything with its colour. Talk about redundant data! Probably, his concern is I will miss "the" train or "the" car he is talking about. Second, it was possible because the car was thrice as big as the train. It was like a pickup car picking up the train to park it elsewhere. I guess the train was parked incorrectly, blocking someone's main gate.

The car and the train are at two different scales. The real world has a fixed scale that always remains the same. The two manufacturers transformed the car and the train to two different scales: kid's world 1 and kid's world 2. I would prefer everything scaled proportionately to only one kid's world. Doing that would give a realistic sense to the kid. Having said that, imagine drawing a picture of a virus scaled further "down" twenty times to match the scaling down of the car to place both things in the same kid's world!

Scaling is an essential concept in machine learning. We usually call it feature scaling, data normalisation, or data standardisation. It is done at a data pre-processing stage to avoid variables with a higher scale impacting the model more than those with a lower scale. A higher-scale variable should not be given any extra importance in the model compared to a lower-scale variable.

Scaling is very useful in distance-based algorithms, gradient descent-based algorithms, and dimension reduction algorithms such as the PCA (Principal Component Analysis). In gradient descent-based algorithms, scaling ensures that the steps for gradient descent are updated at the same rate for all features. Distance-based algorithms such as K-Means Clustering and KNN (K Nearest Neighbours) rely on calculating distances between data points. They are most impacted by different scales of features. Hence, there is a need to perform scaling. PCA selects the components with maximum variance. It should not assume that the direction of maximum variance corresponds to a person's annual salary (compared to the age). It is just that the salary is at a much higher scale than the age as far as numbers are concerned. Scaling reduces the impact of outliers in the dataset.

The two most used scaling techniques are 1) Normalization and 2) Standardization. In normalisation, we rescale all the variables of the dataset to a 0 to 1 range. This is also called min-max scaling. The lower end, the upper end, and the range could be anything. We can choose to rescale our features to a 7 to 12 range or a 100 to 189 range. All features must be rescaled to the same range. This technique is quite frequently used in neural networks. On the other hand, standardisation transforms the values of each variable in the dataset to have a 0 mean and unit variance. This technique is usually used during clustering and PCA.

We must be careful when using terms such as scaling down or scaling up. Some variables need to be scaled up, and a few others need to be scaled down to bring all variables into the same range. Also, note that we can rescale only numeric variables.

A single target scale of the world makes it impossible to show a child a picture of a virus. In addition to solving this practical challenge, multiple kid worlds (World 1 and World 2, as I mentioned at the beginning) do good for one more thing: creativity. How would my mind, fed with forty-one years of continuous "real" inputs, allow me to carry a train on a car? What unnecessary artificial worlds kids live in these days! I despise anything artificial. Oh, AI and Generative AI?

different levels of scaling are essential
    ↳ to represent meaningfully
    ↳ for comprehension

feature scaling
    ↳ normalization
    ↳ standardization
    ↳ data preprocessing stage
    ↳ avoids imbalanced impact from one variable
    ↳ reduces outlier impact

Scaling useful in
    ↳ distance based algorithms
    ↳ gradient descent based algorithms
    ↳ dimensionality reduction algorithms

WAIT, ARE YOU BUILDING A MODEL?

Technical prowess is essential to be a good data scientist. Business and functional knowledge are crucial, too. Technical skills would encapsulate statistical concepts, programming, visualisation, and presentation expertise. A model that does not solve a business problem well but is used frequently to comply with the pressure of adopting analytics is like a cancer to business. On the other hand, a model that provides recommendations well but is not used enough by users due to a lack of sensitisation to the benefits of analytics is a loss of opportunity. Either way, data does not play the pivotal role it should play in giving a competitive advantage to the organisation.

Data science is not machine learning (training the model) alone. It includes all activities from understanding the business problem to finally implementing and monitoring the solution in the live environment. The outcome of this exercise should be an end-to-end solution that could flourish either standalone or in tandem with an existing IT application. Most of the cases I have seen belong to the second category. It might be that I have not seen enough yet. Attributing revenue growth to an analytics solution alone is very tricky. One must be careful to eliminate all other possible revenue boosters. Conversion of a business problem statement to an analytics problem statement is equally tricky.

For example, let us say that the business problem is that the organisation's revenue has decreased consistently over the last four years. Decide on the scope (products, timeline, extent) of the problem by working with the appropriate business teams. In this context, let's assume that the scope is defined. What could be the various possible analytics problem statements? First, identify high-potential products from the list in scope that the sales team can focus on. Selling popular products to someone new will be smoother. Second, identify the high-potential prospects the marketing team could target with customised and personalised campaigns. One could determine what kind of prospects would be easier to convert. Third, arrive at the best market mix. How much should you spend on which channel for the best returns from the marketing campaigns? Allocate the budget where it is the most useful. Fourth, forecast next quarter's sales and alert with recommendations. If the forecast is done at different levels of aggregation (region, store, product category, product, and item), it would be possible to narrow down the entity that is "misbehaving." Fifth, predict ticket resolution times, communicate the same to customers, and improve their experience with the business. An enriched customer experience will ensure winning new customers with less effort.

The above options need to be discussed with business stakeholders. One or more of them should be selected to build a solution on. Each option above has a unique way of increasing revenue. We should be able to quantify the impact of each of the five solutions on revenue and then pick up the top two or three solutions. In addition, nobody stops us from determining the best item (whose sales are about to decrease) to pitch to the best prospect through the most effective marketing channel and ensuring that any ticket raised related to that item is resolved within the promised time. Or should I say, promise the time based on when the resolution can be achieved?

Remember that all five solutions need not cater to the same business team, meaning five teams can come forward simultaneously and show interest. Ranking will help to prioritise. Training a model is not a mandatory activity in a data science project.

You would often encounter situations where an exploratory data analysis (EDA) alone provided the necessary insights. When the business team uses the insights to solve their problem, it becomes an elegant analytics solution.

Provide an end to end solution
    instead of an AIML only solution

one business problem can have
    multiple analytics solutions
        ↳ discuss with business teams
        ↳ Prioritise
        ↳ estimate ROI
        ↳ estimate implementation feasibility

IS AI WORLD A VUCA WORLD?

AIML and generative AI have taken the world by storm. They are here to stay. They are democratising knowledge and access to information and explaining things we never understood earlier. While we talk about the guardrails that must be in place to "tame" them, we cannot ignore the power they give us to create an intelligent, better and equal society.

Volatility. The volatility is caused by diminishing distances among nations, organisations, groups, and individuals. A significant event occurring in one corner of the planet instantly impacts the decisions and activities in the other corner. A few days ago, the news of Meta releasing Llama 3.1 as the most powerful open-source LLM was out. I pushed my plan for the subsequent morning to make space for the new model in my schedule. It is a different thing that I also had to make space in my computer for the three models with 8 billion, 70 billion, and 405 billion parameters. While I was working on it, news came that Mistral released Mistral Large 2 with 123 billion parameters, which performs at par with Llama 3.1 405B. A size of one-third and performance at par is commendable. It makes our lives thrice easier. Don't get surprised because size and performance need not be strictly related. A lot depends on the quality of the training dataset used. Having pushed once, I wonder how far I should move the non-LLM tasks. Yes, the world is volatile. Plans change by the minute. However, have we not been saying that change was the only constant? Now is the time to live the saying.

Uncertainty. We have always been wary of the future. We don't know what will kill us or what might bring an end to the human species. Right. These sound like reasons to be scared. We have loved peeping into our future. At no other time were we better placed to predict than now. With humongous volumes of data and sophisticated tools at our disposal, we understand the past and the present. We use that knowledge to predict our future. You know what I am arriving at. AIML with HITL (Human in the Loop) provides us with the wherewithal to stride towards the future we want.

Complexity. Complexity is the enemy of explainability. The more we understand our actions, decisions, organisations, and the world through data they generate, the less complex they appear. Imagine a doctor prescribing you medication without explaining the disease. This is akin to expecting the business user to accept the recommendations of an ML model lacking explainability.

Ambiguity. Abstraction breeds ambiguity. If you keep abstracting two different entities higher and higher, they will eventually start becoming ambiguous. This is not different from the data aggregation levels data scientists deal with. When you aggregate data weekly, you lose information on days. Similarly, a monthly aggregation loses information on weeks. Anything evolving rapidly brings in a certain amount of ambiguity and lack of structure. I am sure things will be more evident when they become our way of life. The only ambiguity we will be left with is "Haan ke Haan".

AIML is a wonderful weapon in our arsenal to fight volatility, uncertainty, complexity, and ambiguity (VUCA). I would go to the extent of proposing to have a VUCA score for every AIML solution we develop. The score must tell us about the percentage by which the solution reduces the vuca-ism of the world.

Some say we live in a VUCA world these days. I agree that geopolitical dynamics, climate disruptions, unstable economies, and global pandemics are problems that need to be solved. Haven't we been solving problems all this while?

> VUCA
>   ↳ Volatile
>   ↳ Uncertain
>   ↳ Complex
>   ↳ Ambiguous
>
> AI helps reduce VUCAism
>
> Solving Problems has been our way of living life

DO YOU TRUST YOUR AI?

I am the clothes you wear / I protect things you care / Change me not, I am smelly / Value me not, I make you Junglee / Thus says the password. Hoping I am not trusted / Gasping for air with regulators around / Take care bro, meet you next round / Just answering a question unintended / Thus says the LLM hallucination. I am the fence around you / I clean impurities that surround you / You are marvellously built / But missing a stilt / Thus says the guardrail to LLM.

Have you ever taken medicine without understanding from the doctor which disease you are suffering from? The feeling is the same when a data scientist suggests a user follow the machine learning model's recommendation. Enter explainable AI. Is there a way to build such AI systems? Winning the user's trust becomes more essential and challenging when discussing generative AI. As with earlier occasions, let's find out whether I answer or raise more questions!

Clients must trust their service providers with their data. Business users must trust data scientists with machine learning models. Individual users must trust large language models with generated responses. Organisations and regulators must trust LLM benchmarking done by LLM creators. They must trust the built-in LLM guardrails and those designed externally for LLM-powered applications. One must trust the training dataset used for creating the foundational LLMs.

The service provider must explain to customers how their data will be utilised. They must mention the data masking approach and the columns or records to be masked. The data scientist must mention the dataset used for training the ML model and discuss the performance evaluation metrics used to approve the model. The prediction produced by the model should be accompanied by the features influencing the model's overall behaviour and the important factors resulting in a specific prediction. We can name them model-level and prediction-level explainability.

LLM creators must publish details of data used to train base versions of LLMs. The same applies to fine-tuned LLMs, such as instruction-tuned, code-tuned, creative writing-tuned, or medical advice-tuned versions. They must publish the strengths and weaknesses of these models. If done transparently, benchmarking model behaviour with popular LLMs goes a long way to fostering trust in users. Creators must explain steps they have taken to prevent LLMs from generating responses marred with ethical, legal, cultural, or racial violations.

There are quite a few ways developers of LLM-powered applications can build responsibility and accountability into their applications. They can implement checks in prompts and RAG knowledge stores. They can cleanse the responses before displaying them to the user. Developers can introduce checks and monitoring snippets in their source code that interact with LLMs.

The question remains: Would you hand over the decision-making to the machine? I always opine, "Let's hand over neither the decision-making nor the decision-making process to the machine." Use the output or recommendation from the model to make your decision. Effectively, we are turning the model as an input to the decision-making process rather than the decision itself. This concept is called HITL (Human in the Loop). A subject matter expert reviews the model's output and intervenes whenever necessary. I agree there are specific mission-critical decisions where the human-in-the-loop approach is insufficient.

In such scenarios, should we not convert our approach to MITL (Machine in the Loop) instead of HITL? I guess that's what many of the earlier systems started with. We just didn't have a fancy name. Is it not pragmatic to go back a few steps when the user takes time to build confidence in our generative AI solutions?

SECTION B

THE TRIALS:
CHALLENGES IN DATA SCIENCE

Siddharth to Varun: As I grew more confident, I encountered my first big project, which mirrored the challenges that the industry usually faces in this field. These five articles became five formidable obstacles I have overcome, each testing my resolve and pushing me to think creatively.

CHALLENGES OF A DATA SCIENTIST

While the world is going crazy about the possibilities AI and ML (Artificial Intelligence and Machine Learning) have to offer and while we look at our future with excitement, I would like to highlight here the frequent hardships and challenges that a data scientist goes through in his day-to-day work. The intent is not to dampen the party. Instead, it is to acknowledge that there are common problems across the board that need our attention. Solving them will let us party harder!

Deciding which business problems are best solved in the data science way:

Managers often get carried away with the buzz around machine learning and force fit data science solutions to each and every business problem. However, that is not a good practice. Certain business problems could be solved through a simple process improvement, through extra staffing or through an IT application modification. The solutions mentioned above might not require to be solved through a machine learning model building exercise and might even be solved at a lesser cost with higher effectiveness.

Bad quality of data:

Data scientists often have to work through a low volume of data, missing values, outliers and junk values. This calls for a good amount of effort on data preparation. A well-prepared data helps produce better insights and better models. Quite often the historical data used to build a supervised classification model (binary or multiclass) has class imbalance. In such case the event rate of the positive class is very low. This demands that the data scientist either over-sample the minority class or under-sample the majority class or do both to reduce the imbalance before feeding the dataset to the model building algorithm.

Encountering new classes during prediction:

There are times when the training dataset does not have a particular class of one of the feature variables. In cases where the missing class appears during prediction in real life, the prediction fails. In order not to end up with such a problem, data scientists often choose a larger train dataset and a smaller test dataset expecting all possible classes of all feature variables are included for training. Another approach is to carry out a stratified sampling while creating the training dataset. This ensures that all classes occur at least once in the training dataset.

Selecting the most useful metric for model evaluation:

For each of the regression, classification and unsupervised modelling techniques, there are multiple model evaluation metrics that need to be considered before approving a model to be ready for production. Quite often, the model clears few metrics and does not clear the rest making it difficult for a final approval decision. One way of handling this ambiguity is to rank order the metrics in terms of criticality and ensure that all top metrics are good for the model. It should be fine to fail the not so critical metrics. As a best practice the rank ordering should be done before building the baseline model. In addition, along with deciding which metric is critical, a data scientist should also pre-decide what should be acceptable values of that metric so that an appropriate threshold could be set.

Premature celebration in case of high technical performance:

A data scientist should always focus on the actual real-life outcome the ML model brings for solving the business problem. Examples of real-life successful outcomes could be providing a better customer experience, higher Net Promoter Score (NPS), increasing revenue, saving cost, increasing demand for a product or making operations smoother and faster. Real-life performance is the king. Not the technical performance before using the solution in a live environment.

Effort estimation of data science projects:

It often becomes quite difficult to correctly estimate the time and effort required to first deploy the data science solution in a live environment and then to achieve the Return on Investment (ROI) from the improved business process. This mainly results from the nature of exercises that are carried out in such projects. Machine learning model building is highly experimental in nature, and one may arrive at the best model by working on and discarding an unknown number of options and models.

Attributing a positive business outcome to a Data Science solution:

What portion of the ROI is due to the newly deployed data science solution and what portion is due to other factors that have taken place independent of the data science solution? Not an easy task to determine! The industry knows that there is definite value addition from AI and ML solutions. However, quantifying the value addition is something we have to be clearer on.

High number of classes of a categorical feature variable:

Models perform weakly when the number of distinct values of a categorical variable is too high. For example, in many cases 50 such distinct values (classes) would be considered a high number. One way to handle this scenario is by bucketing the 50 distinct values further into 8 classes (let's say) and hence making it manageable.

In conclusion, standardising the process of executing a data science project through best practices will definitely lead to mitigating some of the challenges mentioned above. At the same time, be wary of standardising the process so much that there is little room left for out of the box thinking and innovation. After all, innovation is what has primarily defined the field of AI and ML for humankind.

CUSTOMER NOT A STATISTIC

Looking at data (observations, variables, datasets) day in and day out makes me quite data-centric. So much so that when I got introduced to my colleagues on the floor at my new job, I requested them to tell me in "summary statistics" how many years of work experience they had, how far they lived from the office, which parts of India they came from, what their educational backgrounds looked like, and what they liked doing in their free time. We did laugh at the approach. But I got what I wanted. I got it at the appropriate aggregation level. However, did I miss anything? Yes. If nothing else, I missed the human touch. They were hardly ten in number.

We model customer behaviour to predict whether customers will buy our products and services. I have often pondered how correct we are in converting customer behaviour into statistics. A behaviour resulting from an individual's "local" mood and "global" personality, among many other factors such as upbringing, schooling and whatnot. Was the customer quite upset with his boss at the office when he received your email to fill out the feedback survey form? How do we track that? Is the customer's purchase behaviour so unpredictable that any degree of generalisation through an equation between features and target variables is insufficient to predict? Or do you end up making the model so generic that it loses its usefulness in action-ability? In B2B scenarios, too, it mostly boils down to individuals making the final decision. I have never seen any variables related to the customer's mood or personality stored in an organisation's databases. Honestly speaking, it's not possible either to model customer behaviour completely. You bring me an ML model built with an exhaustive set of variables. I will tell you two more that you have missed.

The best ways to deal with this lack of perfection in recommendations produced by ML models are 1) Ensure that recommendations are non-intrusive while respecting the years of experience the decision maker has, 2) Make the ML model as explainable as possible, and 3) Leave the final decision to be made by the decision maker.

I am not pessimistic about the potential of AIML to solve our problems. I look at the future with as much excitement as you do. I intend that we should know what we cannot make AIML do for us. I have been vocal about it during interactions with college students, too, on multiple occasions. Students often look at industry practitioners for the proper guidance and transparency of what works and what doesn't.

The question I am raising is – Is artificial intelligence making us too artificial? We even talk about developing synthetic respondents for surveys to get "customer" feedback on an organisation's products, services, support, sales process and call center touch points. By doing this, we have effectively sent the customer (one in the flesh, blood, and with a personality) out of the loop and agreed that the survey design, survey response, analysis, insight generation, and recommendations would be instantaneous without human involvement. My only question is how accurate it is. Among my maze of thoughts, are two suggestions too that can help get the best out of synthetic respondents. One is to use synthetic respondents and real customer respondents in parallel for few months or quarters while comparing how much they match or differ from each other. The second is to always keep augmenting the real customer responses with synthetic ones and never let go of the advantages we get from real customer feedback.

As I have already said, I am immensely passionate about AIML. At the same time, I don't have the habit of doing something just because my neighbour is doing it (except when I took the entrance exams for both engineering and medical, hoping one of them would work). Tell me about childhood dreams and them coming true!

effectiveness of capturing customer
behaviour in a model
human touch in analysis
best practices
    ↳ non intrusive recommendations
    ↳ explainable models
    ↳ decision made by human being

FOR WHOEVER THOUGHT DATA SCIENTISTS KNEW CHURN PREDICTION

Ihave learned three things over time: 1) Just because an excuse is correct doesn't make it any less of an excuse 2) More value is added to a discussion by asking the right questions than by giving the right answers 3) You cannot say half of the job is done in stand-up comedy by just standing up. I am a little carried away by the second one today. I am going to discuss the topic of churn analytics by only asking questions. You tell me whether the questions guide you in the right direction.

How do we define a churn so that we identify exactly how many and when churns have happened in the past? Is it the event when the status of the customer was updated as inactive in the IT system? Would defining churn with a reduction in product or service usage by more than a threshold number be more helpful? Is it when the customer didn't make his bill payments for several consecutive months? What signals or patterns are more likely to occur in case of customers about to churn? How do patterns differ among customers who are not at risk of churn? Should we consider churn a binary event (churn, no churn) or a multi-level event with various churn gradations?

How much in advance should we predict churn? How much lead time does the business team need to act on at-risk customers? What offers or campaigns suit a customer predicted to churn in 3 months?

What urgent incentives do you offer a customer predicted to churn next week? Is it ok to let specific customers churn? Should we consider a customer's lifetime value (LTV) prediction to decide how much criticality to assign to save the customer? How do we calculate the effectiveness of a churn prediction? If the customer is predicted to churn but doesn't, is it a good churn prevention action or a bad prediction? Isn't it always a wrong prediction if the customer is not predicted to churn but churns? Don't you think because the customer was considered to be not at risk, no action was taken?

How does a customer's journey look till the point of churn? Does that give us a good peep into the factors causing churn? Was the outcome of a customer touch point with the organisation negative? How many touch points went negative for a customer? Which channels (automated IVR, call centre, mobile app, website, stores, in-person interaction, SMS, email, WhatsApp) mattered more in influencing churn? On average, have we taken more time to solve tickets for customers who eventually churned compared to those who didn't? Were quantitative responses to customer survey questions harsher from customers who churned? Was the sentiment derived from a qualitative response negative from a customer who churned? Does churn increase with decreasing NPS and vice versa?

Which product and service areas have a higher churn rate? How does the tenure of customers correlate with the churn rate? Are new customers more likely to churn compared to older ones? Customers who have a higher frequency of touch points churn more or less? Did the customer have a good experience during onboarding? What does the trend of churn rate look like? Is there any seasonality? Is there any other pattern in the movement? How many times has the customer defaulted on bill payments?

Should we design the churn problem as a binary classification problem or a multi-class classification problem? Before building a churn prediction model, should we cluster the customers first into different groups through an unsupervised learning technique? Which influencers of churn can be controlled (for example, customer experience)? Which influencers of churn are outside the organisation's control (for example, economic slowdown)? When I say something impacts churn negatively, isn't it ambiguous? Instead, shouldn't I say something decreases the churn rate or something reduces the churn numbers? Shouldn't I be clear on whether new customer additions offset churn numbers? Or is churn calculation independent of how many new customers the organisation has added? Are churn numbers and churn rates calculated on a monthly frequency? Half-yearly? Annually? What is the target reduction in churn rate through this prediction solution? Do we know how much monetary savings it translates to if we reduce churn by the target rate?

DATA GAVE NOTHING

Once upon a time, the gossip in the town was that Mr. Rastogi's daughter seemed to have a thing for Rahul. These days, it would be, "You know, Sanjana, the data scientist, spent four days and found nothing from the data. Not a single actionable insight. What use!"

The biggest challenge of working from home is not having to decide alone whether the text box in the GUI (Graphical User Interface) is positioned correctly. Instead, it is to shut the door behind me, stopping my two-year-old son from entering the room. Emotional challenge. Financial challenges, by themselves, never hurt. They transform into emotional ones before hurting. A data scientist often encounters a similar difficulty (in type and not extent). There are passionate data scientists. The problem happens when they attach emotionally to the data, an ML model, or the expected outcome. Data scientists go the extra mile to prove that data exploration, model building, model evaluation, and prediction are worth their salt.

If the best solution to a business problem does not stay in data, we should be open about it. A data scientist should narrate the story data has to say, not the story the business team wants to hear. Data stands for truth, and let the data scientist also stand for the same truth. Let the truth be told if the data science team has spent some budget understanding the business problem, exploring data, and coming up with a finding that's not music to the business team's ears. Charts on the slides need not look visually appealing. They must be factually correct.

I want to convey to data scientists not to be emotionally attached to your data, ML model, or ML solution. Be ready to discard a big chunk of your analysis and conclude that this data said nothing. Be prepared to start all over again. The "restart" strategy works not for UPSC exams alone. We restarted when there was an earthquake, a cyclone, or a flood. In the data science world, getting an accuracy of 33% for your baseline ML model (the first basic one you build) is earth-shattering, if not an earthquake.

One should be on the path to building the right thing first before trying to build the thing right. A common bias I observe in the data science process is a data scientist sticking to and highlighting the model evaluation metrics in which the model does well and ignoring the other metrics. I prefer to keep my remarks vague with "doing well/not doing well" rather than "pass/fail" because we often forget to set the performance threshold for a metric beforehand. This leads to a changing goalpost problem (even unintentionally) while evaluating the model's merit. In such a case, the ML model is sometimes fantabulous, sometimes good, but never underperforming. Much like the colleagues who know how to talk! To clarify, the threshold of a metric does not stay the same across all use cases. Based on which business problem we are solving, the threshold changes. Sometimes, we might be ok with bulging false positives. At other times, with a high false negative percentage.

Patterns identified from data should be actionable. Instead, I should say insights derived from those patterns identified from the data should be actionable. An insight that the business teams cannot use for solving their problem goes nowhere more than confirming that the data scientist has good presentation skills (both creating slides and explaining). I don't discount that the data gets processed from raw to insightful with unmatchable love and care from the data scientist. However, don't be heartbroken when you must tell twenty people on a conference call, "This data gave nothing. Restart."

getting emotionally attached to models

data based solution vs. non data solutions

be open to restart

actionable insight vs. non actionable insight

HAVE YOU STUDIED YOUR GLASS OF LASSI ENOUGH?

I have often wondered how we end up being what we are. How do we end up doing what we are doing now? I mean precisely now. Why am I typing these words?

This moment is preceded by countless decision moments in the past. Most decisions are made at a subconscious level without any planning. Picture this. Last evening, I decided to have a sweet lassi instead of coffee at my favourite restaurant. I feel a little lazy and sleepy while missing the regular dose of caffeine. I sleep early and wake up late. Hence, instead of writing an article last night that leads the world to build the next LLM demonstrating AGI (Artificial General Intelligence), I am writing on a dumb and abstract subject. What an opportunity loss! And because of what – my seemingly harmless and trivial decision of choosing lassi over coffee. Don't you think I "decided" to go to the restaurant last evening only because three years ago, I bought this wonderful four-wheeler? I might not have driven to the restaurant at all otherwise. I purchased this vehicle in the first place because I "chose" to answer a data science-related question impressively in my last interview. I realise that a seemingly desirable demonstration of brilliance in answering the interviewer's question has deprived the world of AGI and me of "father of AGI" status. What an opportunity loss!

A few questions arise. 1) How far back can I keep going like this? 2) What is a unit decision moment? Especially when most of them are made subconsciously. 3) Is the "decision moment" a continuous or categorical variable? 4) Is it possible to track the path and trend of decision moments per individual? 5) Is it possible to plan and "intervene" in someone's path of decision moments? 6) It seems evident that my earlier decision moments severely affected my current state. Moreover, the paths of decision moments of others affect mine. Would you agree? 7) How can I determine whether all decisions I have taken in the past have been the best set unless I see what my end state looks like? Remember my impressive performance in my last interview? Does it mean I should wait till I see my EOL (end of life) to decide if I should start celebrating?

In short, my thought is, can AIML model success? In a broader sense, can AIML model a successful life? I want to be recommended precise actions I must take in the next two hours that could lead me to get promoted in my organisation to the next role within the next three months. However, at the same time, I don't want to meet with a fatal road accident in the fourth month while driving to the office for a meeting of all recently promoted employees! Would AIML offer me options while I am mindful of the pros and cons? Most likely, an unpromoted employee is better than a promoted dead employee!

While I know my path of decision moments, I do not know the countless paths I skipped. They never happened. I am curious to know about them. Can AIML help me find those by learning from the paths of everyone we have ever known on the planet? If yes, and if intervention is possible, we are looking at a human race consisting of regular, boring, successful individuals. Wouldn't you instead prefer not to "predict-control" your future and allow the excitement of the uncertainty? Someone said that ignorance was bliss.

Knowing the ill effects of a glass of lassi is undoubtedly overwhelming. I have had countless glasses of lassi in my life. Are you in control of your glass of lassi? Human beings' desire to control things is harmfully insatiable. We try to control nature, destiny, and lives. We want to be all-powerful. While I say with power comes responsibility, I would also say with ignorance comes bliss.

cause and effect
which decision leads to which ones?
opportunity loss
questions related to the cause/effect chain

can success be modelled?
can success be architectured?

SECTION C

THE ASCENT:
CAREER IN DATA SCIENCE

Siddharth to Varun: Overcoming the challenges caught the eye of senior management. The seven articles below parallel my climb up the corporate ladder, with each article representing a new role or responsibility I take on.

SKILLS REQUIRED
IN DATA SCIENCE TEAMS

Initially, I thought I would be safe not suggesting an effort distribution across various phases of a data science project. But then what good is an author who looks for such kind of safety nets? In a typical data science project, approximately 30 per cent of the effort of the data science team (not talking about data engineering, governance, and ML Ops teams) goes into data identification and data preparation, 20 per cent for data exploration, another 30 per cent for model building and evaluation, and 20 per cent for creating presentation content with visualisations and explanation to business teams. I would say the last 20 per cent also includes the effort required for providing inputs to other data teams such as data engineering, data governance and ML Ops. I am assuming that interactions between the data science and business teams can occur in any of the above phases while still holding the effort distribution as mentioned above. I am discussing skills in a team instead of skills of a data scientist because the skills absent in one individual can be compensated with the availability of those skills in other individuals in the team.

People say they are "data people" while introducing themselves. I assume they have a good data orientation. Do you prefer saying that you are delayed by a few minutes, and you will reach soon or that you are delayed by 20 minutes? Do you leave your communication subject to interpretation or anchor it with unambiguous data points? The data scientist should be a data detective. With investigative thinking at the core, they should always ask "why". Why does a pattern look the way it does? Why is there a difference or similarity between two variables, two observations or even two datasets? A data scientist should be able to uncover stories that the data tell. They should understand that the difference in intensity between medium and low is not the same as that between high and medium. However, high is greater than medium, which is greater than low (ordinal categorical variable). So on and so forth.

A data science team should have a greenfield exploration ability and be open to discovery and change of track of analysis. Every decision during a project should be based on data, not emotions. The data science team requires visualisation expertise. Data should be represented in graphs and charts highlighting the areas that lead to observations, which, in turn, lead to insights. The team should have good presentation skills, which include preparing the content to be presented to stakeholders and explaining the content. Based on the primary audience, the team should be able to simplify technical details into consumable ideas. The message should be precise and complete.

Expertise in Machine Learning (ML) programming languages such as R, SAS and Python is necessary. The team spends much time writing SQL queries to interact with databases. Expertise in SQL is essential. More often than not the team has to program the data capture, data preparation, data exploration, ML model training, and model evaluation processes. A critical expectation from the data science team these days is to provide appropriate explainability of the analytics solution. Users want to know why the model recommends the way it does. Which factor, among many others, played the role of a powerful influencer in the decision-making that led to a specific prediction or recommendation?

The team must make sense of the deluge of chaotic information available online and from other sources. With ease of access to knowledge, one should know how to get the maximum productivity from the limited resources available to us (time and effort). The team should learn not only how to apply the ML algorithms but also the concepts behind those algorithms. That demands a good hold on the subject of statistics. Strong domain knowledge and business acumen are necessary to create a technology-based solution that solves a business problem. If I have to conclude with a summary, then I would say the knowledge of a data science team should include 1) ML algorithms, 2) Statistics, 3) Programming, 4) SQL, 5) Domain, and 6) Presentation.

PREREQUISITES FOR RUNNING A DATA SCIENCE PROJECT

Is historical data available for building a data science solution? Does data attest to the business problem? In other words, is there a metric that highlights the business problem? I will go slightly off track with a general belief in the industry. What if no metric is captured to quantify the extent of the business problem? For example, there could be an obvious "sense" that there are customer complaints now and then in how troubleshooting tickets related to a particular home appliance are handled. The data scientist proposes to implement a ticket-closure-time prediction ML model based on the various features related to customer demographics, the ticket, the device, device usage, the customer's financial status, and competition in the market. This predicted time to resolution is proposed to be communicated to the customer at regular intervals till the ticket is closed. This is aimed at reducing customer dissatisfaction. Remember that we have all the data related to training the model: the features and the target variable (time to resolution). We don't have the extent of the current dissatisfaction level or to what extent the current dissatisfaction level will go down after using the data science solution. However, you are sure that the dissatisfaction level will go down. Now tell me whether you would go ahead with this proposal. I am not answering this question today.

I will align more with the industry in the rest of the article. We should have historical data to solve a business problem using data analytics. No data, no data science. Sometimes, I wonder why we call it "historical" data. Data points, by default, represent events in the past. In a way, real-time data is also historical. The event has taken place, and hence, you have real-time data. Usually, business teams conduct a cost-benefit analysis to ensure the analytics solution has an acceptable ROI (Return on Investment). In the scenario I mentioned initially, a correct ROI cannot be calculated unless you "quantify" the extent of customer dissatisfaction reduced.

The essential prerequisite of entering a data science project is that we should be able to convert the business problem statement into an analytics problem statement, which we can call an "analytics solution statement", to be precise. There is no overarching analytics problem statement. When you try to define one, it becomes a solution statement instead of a problem statement. A business problem statement could be, "The percentage of customers complaining about how troubleshooting tickets are handled is increasing". The analytics solution statement could be, "Predict and communicate to the customer regularly the time remaining for resolving his/her ticket". However, I agree that you can continue asking "why" to the business problem at multiple intermediate levels and might want to call each of them an analytics problem to be solved. One business problem can have more than one analytics solution. In such a case, the data science team should agree with the business team on the best analytics solution and go ahead with it. If more than one analytics solution should be implemented, then the order of priority should be decided by taking inputs from the business team.

Do we have the expertise and skills (machine learning algorithms, statistics, domain experience, presentation, data engineering, data governance, MLOps, and programming) required to execute the data science project? Do we have the software and hardware available with us in line with the software and hardware requirements? This could depend on the volume of data and the types (structured, unstructured) of data we will deal with. Do we understand who the solution's end consumer will be? Will it be used by the sales team, marketing, ordering, finance, logistics, HR, IT or the service assurance team? Do we have an idea of how the solution might be consumed?

Possibilities could be as a flat file report, full-fledged dashboard in an application, single field displaying the predicted number on an existing screen, and so on. An important consideration is the estimated adoption of the solution by business users and the rate at which adoption is assumed to increase over the months following the implementation. This would determine the success of the solution and indicate what ROI we can expect. Teams arrived at quantified benefits without factoring in the lack of adoption. In that case, they assume 100% adoption right from the day of implementation, which is false. Ever!

Lastly, we should know who is paying for the solution. I expect that the sponsor will be super serious about the quality of the solution. All teams collaborating to solve the business problem are answerable to the sponsor at the end of the day. My author friend raised an interesting question in his book. Let's consider that five projects are lined up in an organisation's AI program with a decreasing order of priority. They are from five different departments (functions). The projects often will have overlapping data requirements. Hence, there is a need for overlapping data engineering requirements. It is easy to see that the project that runs first will have to bear the highest expense of the total data engineering work. In a practical scenario, why should the first sponsor spend extra for subsequent sponsors? Should the additional cost of the first project come from the CIO budget? A valid point to think about.

checklist to start DS Project
   ↳ historical data
   ↳ data attesting the Problem
   ↳ cost benefit analysis
   ↳ business Problem statement
     Converting to analytics Problem statement
   ↳ expertise and skills
   ↳ s/w and h/w
   ↳ solution's end customer
   ↳ consumption approach
   ↳ estimated adoption
   ↳ sponsor

THE MAGICAL INGREDIENTS OF AN OUTSTANDING DATA SCIENTIST

This week, I addressed a batch of thirty students getting inducted into a two-year MS program in data science. In my quest to give my audience the maximum value for their time, I spoke about what makes a data scientist successful. This article is an amalgamation of what I said there and what I want to tell you in addition.

Understand the business context and the ecosystem. What business problem are we solving? Does it help the organisation achieve its goals? Is AI ML the right tool for solving this problem? Understand where AI should stop and human review should step in. We often go overboard in automating and handing the steering wheel to AI. I guess it is essential to understand that we deal with human beings with their levels of confidence and reasons for apprehension. Use AI ML to innovate responsibly and with fairness. For example, have you thought about how the creators of training data for large language models should be compensated? Have a system to hear back problems from colleagues, clients, and the industry. Have an action plan to handle issues arising from your AI

ML solutions. Focus on explainability. Improve explainability if necessary.

AI ML requires creativity and thinking out of the box. You will probably believe me better when you envisage the possibilities of a generative AI-based future of AI ML. Or should I say a generative AI-based future of humankind? Naysayers might require a bit more convincing than this. Therefore, I would rather be biased toward action and not biased toward ideas. I don't blame them. My favourite comparison is that you cannot say half of the job is done in stand-up comedy by just standing up. The data science community has just stood up. The jokes are yet to be delivered with all the story build-ups and the punch lines.

Data science is the application of concepts and the concepts themselves. The scope is so enormous that the application of concepts becomes a science by itself. One must appreciate the mathematics, statistics, and algorithms that work behind the scenes.

The availability of AI ML knowledge sources is varied, fast and unorganised. At a time when the whole world is experimenting, even the ground truth shifts rapidly. Keeping pace with the developments becomes critical. Specific attributes of an individual that I find helpful in the current scenario are making sense of the chaos, skimming through pages and pages of content, proper prioritisation, and not keeping something aside for the best available time slot. For a reason, one's to-do folder containing PDFs, documents, and the notepad carrying links to articles and videos keeps growing.

There is never a destination. The next destination you aim for is a path to the subsequent destination. Hence, a better idea is to keep enjoying the journey. Nothing attests to this more than the current state of AI. If you consider Generative AI your destination, you should wait for when AGI (Artificial General Intelligence) comes in its complete avatar.

I want to say this without referring to the T-shaped and V-shaped skills the industry discusses. My take on the need of the hour is that it is tough for a data scientist to work only on building ML models. Or someone else is working only on data exploration and another on data collection, cleaning, and preparation. This arrangement does not make sense anymore. It might be it has never made sense in the data science world. An ML expert (who should ideally be building, evaluating, and finalising models) cannot expect a neatly prepared dataset to be available on a silver platter. I am trying to emphasise that a good data scientist should not be blind to data engineering, MLOps, data governance, application development, and data security aspects of the "solution-building chain".

qualities of a successful data scientist
- understanding business context
- understanding tech and people ecosystem
- Is AIML right?
- human in the loop
- creativity and out of box thinking
- strong in concepts and their application
- making sense of chaotic inflow of information
- V shaped skillset
- aware of the solution building chain

CITIZEN DATA SCIENCE DEVELOPER

My friend asked me today if I could explain the difference between development and coding in the IT industry. She was worried that it was a silly question to ask. It was not. The best way I could answer was the development that you do without coding is citizen development. It was unsurprising because I was in the middle of writing this piece. Citizen development might sound fancy. However, it is not yet a foolproof practice. It is believed that the primary advantage of someone being a citizen developer is him/her having a solid domain and industry knowledge while being able to use Low Code No Code (LCNC) platforms to develop business applications. Can I call them business technologists who bridge the gap between business understanding and technical acumen?

I have always believed that data science solutions can be better clustered by functions (departments) than by industries (domains). Marketing analytics, for example, remains more or less the same for finance or manufacturing industries (identifying the target audience for receiving a specific marketing communication). Call centre analytics rests on the same foundational approaches and use cases in all industries. I am not downplaying the role of domain knowledge in building analytics solutions. One cannot solve a problem without understanding how the industry and the organisation work. When discussing the development and implementation of data science solutions by citizen developers, we derive most of our confidence from the domain and function knowledge.

I have always felt that business problems need to be addressed faster than the speed of IT development. I don't mind speaking openly about the most common frustration of business teams towards the IT team. This is more so with data science teams because much of their work is experimental. Experiments fail, we learn, collect and prepare data again, rebuild ML models, and re-evaluate model performance. Finally, after the solution is implemented in the production environment, we discover that adoption is pathetic for various reasons (bad UI, resistance to change). How do we help ease the classic chicken/egg problem of ROI vs. adoption?

I can't harp enough while saying that our focus on the business problem we are solving should be laser-sharp. How does a citizen strategist, a citizen problem solver, or a citizen doctor sound to you? Can we citizen-ise them? Don't be a guy who knows how to ask ChatGPT the next block of code but does not know where to place it in the program. You don't even have to ask if it is an AI pair programming tool such as GitHub Copilot. It suggests without asking. Not the list of methods available as soon as you type the object name, but the complete block of code that should appear next. A quick Google search on citizen "coders" fills the search results containing details of citizen "developers". ChatGPT had a better response, almost in line with my thought of a citizen coder using tools like GitHub Copilot to code. Don't you think we are moving closer to AGI (Artificial General Intelligence)? I believe using a programming copilot to code still falls outside the scope of a citizen developer.

The effort one must put into reviewing a citizen developer's code and the risks associated with incorrect functionalities are humongous. Functionality "breaking" is a better scenario than functionality working incorrectly. The former is easily identifiable, while the latter is not. Imagine citizen development has led to offering a 10% additional discount on average while not winning additional deals or improving customer experience. It will demand strong review measures to be implemented to prevent such minor-looking, highly impacting inaccuracies. Standardised processes, best practices, coaching, and review measures will help mitigate the risks associated with citizen development. People argue that citizen development saves costs. How much of it is offset by the cost of review or overshot by the cost of reviewing and fixing errors in production?

In the Generative AI world, every content creator is a citizen content creator! My apologies if I sounded harsh. I have stopped quipping these days that I have come up with today's TOI article "effortlessly". They might assume I have used ChatGPT. Abstraction is a tricky thing. I call it Helps Loudly Kills Silently (HLKS). Abstraction hides the principles of coding, functions, parameter passing, variable declaration, classes, objects (instance of a class), methods, instance variables, loops, iterations, breaks and whatnot. Yes, ChatGPT helps. Yes, Google search helps. However, you should know what to look for and how good what you find is.

developing vs. coding
citizen developer
    ↳ domain strength
    ↳ fluency with low code no code tools
    ↳ bussiness technologists
function wise vs. domain wise DS usecases
ROI vs. adoption
citizen strategist ?
citizen problem solver ?
citizen doctor ?
Review of citizen developer's output
Saves lost ?
citizen content creator in the Gen AI world

WHEN A DATA SCIENTIST BLABBERS

4, 3.6, 5.4, 5.8, 6, 6.1, 6.2, 5.3, 18. These could be the heights of 9 people in feet among the audience. Height of 18 feet? Sounds unlikely. This is an outlier in the series of 9 numbers. Does the outlier distort the central tendency severely? Yes, if you are interested in the mean height. No, if you are planning to use the median height. Median is the middle value in a set of numbers when arranged either in increasing or decreasing order. It is easy to note that the mean depends on each person's "quantity" of height. In contrast, the median depends just on the "position" of each person's height (to the left or right of the median). The height of 18 feet has no more significant impact than 6 feet because both are to the right of the median (5.8 feet).

A moment here, a moment there / A moment found nowhere / I know I am uninvited / Replace me or ignore me / Am the data scientist's nightmare / Thus, says the value missing

Most of the machine learning algorithms and functions we use do not appreciate the presence of missing values. They must be treated in our dataset. By treated, I mean either removed or replaced, depending on the volume of such missing values. It also depends on where the missing values occur. Do they appear in variables that we are highly interested in or in not-so-critical variables?

I influence you, I change you / I improve you, I worsen you / You need me, you pamper me / You go wrong, when I am wrong / Thus, says the variable independent

The set of independent variables impacts the target variable. The choice of such variables makes or breaks a machine learning model. Too many of them overfit the model, while too few of them underfit. Hence, the set of independent variables should be complete and precise at the same time.

I tried too much, I learnt too much / Don't feed me data unseen / I may not bring justice / To the story nice / Not once, not twice, but thrice / Thus, says the model over-fitted

When the model learns and follows the observations in the training dataset quite strictly, it overfits. In other words, it does not know what to say when given unseen data and asked to predict.

I say the future, I cut the clutter / Feed me historical data, I am hungry / Feed me stale data I am angry / Use your intuition, I serve you well / Trust me blind, I make you fail / Thus, says the model ML

This brings me to stress that we cannot ignore the human-in-the-loop structure of a data science solution. The power to make the final decision should rest in the hands of humans. A data science solution should not "dictate" decisions. It can recommend. It can suggest. It can highlight newer approaches to looking at things. But it cannot replace a human decision-maker.

I say truth, I stand for truth / You cry when I am too small / You cry when I am too big / Use me not I don't speak / Treat me well I tell a story / With all its natural glory / Thus, says the data divine

Needless to say, data has been of supreme importance. Businesses use data to understand customers, products, marketing campaigns, competitors, and whatnot. We use outcomes from data in our everyday lives. Whether we know it or not, whether it is ethical or not, and whether it is a breach of privacy or not are different stories. Data is the king. Or should I say the queen (we celebrated Women's Day yesterday)? Data is the chief. We will keep talking.

Basic data science concepts
→ outliers
→ missing values
→ independent variables
→ over fitted model
→ ML model
→ data

CRACKING A MACHINE
LEARNING INTERVIEW

It looks like the season for upskilling, reskilling, and job-switching, not necessarily in that order. I would say the following if asked to talk about machine learning in 649 words or 863 tokens. Of course, I am taking a leaf out of the book of LLMs when I say tokens.

How do you make a machine learn? You provide input records containing features (often multiple) and one target variable. The ML algorithm determines the best approximate relationship between the features and the target. The object where the relationship is stored mathematically is called an ML model. In the future, the saved model will be used to predict the value of the target when features are provided. As simple as that. When I am on the other side (presumably the powerful side, which should not be the case if the candidate knows that they have all rights to assess the company through the interviewer) of the table, and you explain this difference between an algorithm and a model, you are half-way there. My bias towards this understanding is there because I have seen this concept butchered repeatedly.

Supervised learning occurs when an ML model, such as the one mentioned above, is built through the training process. Each record having a features-target pair is an "example" of what has happened in the past. Unsupervised learning occurs when you stop calling the target as the event output and consider it one of the features, and you use algorithms to "discover" patterns. Hence, in unsupervised learning, we don't have "examples" even though the dataset might be precisely the same as we had in our case of supervised learning. Hence, our dataset is the same, while the treatment is of two types (supervised and unsupervised). If you explain this, you are almost there.

Supervised learning could be achieved through classification (categorical target variable) or regression (continuous target variable) techniques. Logistic regression, decision trees, random forests, KNN, SVM, and ANN are examples of classification algorithms. Classification model evaluation metrics include the confusion matrix, overall accuracy, AUC, ROC, KS statistic, gains table, gains chart, F1 score, precision, and recall. Linear regression, decision trees, random forests, and ANN are examples of regression algorithms. I called them "algorithms" to harp on the fact that what you get from using them is a reusable model for prediction. R square, adjusted R square, RMSE, and MAPE are regression model evaluation metrics. Unsupervised learning occurs when you use clustering, association mining, or dimensionality reduction (such as PCA) algorithms. If you have a GitHub account with compelling examples of usage of the above algorithms, then nothing like it.

Don't forget to talk about how you used non-complex and non-computation-hogging SQL queries to interact with databases. Did I mention only SQL? Please add NoSQL databases and queries to that. Deep learning is an example of an ML algorithm. The large language model (LLM) is an example of a deep learning model and, hence, an example of an ML model. To have our deal straight, LLM is an example of a generative AI model, too. This means that we have the non-LLM type of generative AI. However, they are no match for LLMs, hence our obsession.

No amount of machine learning knowledge is complete without data exploration techniques. One must know how to analyse univariate continuous and categorical variables. The same goes for bivariate continuous and categorical variables. Mention the names of charts (you can call them tools) used in the above six cases (two univariate and four bivariate).

All the above algorithms are non-temporal by nature. Whether row number 20 occurred after row 15 or before does not matter. Before bidding goodbye, say hi to the temporal algorithms called the time series algorithms. Autoregressive (AR), Moving Average (MA), Autoregressive Moving Average (ARMA), Autoregressive Integrated Moving Average (ARIMA), Exponential Smoothing (ES), and Holt-Winters are examples of time series algorithms.

Talk about your captivating storytelling skills in representing complex technical content in simple and easily understandable messages. I skipped talking about all the statistics needed for machine learning work. If I write everything this week, what will I write next week? To be honest, it is the word limit. Or should I say the token limit?

interview topics ML
↳ making machines learn
↳ ML algorithm vs. ML model
↳ supervised vs. unsupervised learning
↳ classification and regression techniques
↳ examples of ML algorithms
↳ evaluation metrics
↳ dimensionality reduction techniques
↳ Github account
↳ optimized sql queries
↳ nosql databases and queries
↳ deep learning and LLMs
↳ generative AI vs. LLMs
↳ data exploration techniques
↳ univariate vs. bivariate analysis
↳ continuous vs. categorical variables
↳ graphs
↳ non temporal vs. temporal data
↳ time series algorithms
        ↳ AR
        ↳ MA
        ↳ ARMA
        ↳ ARIMA
        ↳ exponential smoothing
        ↳ Holt Winters
↳ storytelling

CRACKING AN INTERVIEW
IN STATISTICS FOR ML

Empirical data is gathered through systematic experimentation and observation. We summarise and describe the nature of a dataset through descriptive statistics using charts and tables. We check the central tendency for each variable through mean, median, and mode. In addition, we check their dispersion through variance and standard deviation. We check their distribution. We make predictions and generalisations about the population from a sample of data through inferential statistics. Effectively, we draw conclusions beyond the available data. Hence, descriptive statistics are factual, while inferential statistics involve uncertainty and probability.

The use of descriptive statistics in Machine Learning (ML) is not hard to understand. Data scientists perform descriptive statistical activities to get a firm hold on the data before training ML models. We often build our models on sample data and interpret the results to develop business team recommendations. We can extend these findings from a "sample of the population" to the "population" because of the validity of inferential statistics. This validity is established through the Central Limit Theorem (CLT), which is the cornerstone of Machine Learning. As per the CLT, the distribution of sample means (called sampling distribution) is approximately normal. The larger the size of the samples, the more normal and narrower the sampling distribution becomes. This holds irrespective of the distribution of the same variable in the original population. The real power of the CLT lies in the fact that we don't need to know the distribution of the population in advance. It need not be normal. An ML expert trains a model on a sample dataset and uses it to make predictions for the whole population. The entire population is nothing but any combination of the input variables we provide our model in the future for carrying out a prediction. As simple as that. It's probably as elusive, too, as that.

Hypothesis testing in machine learning is used to determine whether there is enough evidence in a sample of data to infer that a particular condition is valid for the entire population. The null hypothesis is the default assumption. If the null hypothesis is rejected, we accept the alternative hypothesis. We determine statistical significance using a threshold commonly set at 0.05 (5%). We reject the null hypothesis if the p-value is less than the significance level. Chi-Square test, t-test, and ANOVA are examples of hypothesis tests.

Non-parametric hypothesis tests don't need the data to be normally distributed. They often work on medians as the central tendency. On the other hand, parametric hypothesis tests of means require the data to be normally distributed. We are good because we have our friendly Central Limit Theorem. Examples of such tests are t-tests, one-way ANOVA, etc. Can you guess which scenarios have a median working better as a central tendency representation than a mean? Say hi to our troublesome outliers. However, if the sample size is considerably large, we would use one of the parametric tests instead.

A loss function quantifies the error between the predicted and observed target values. It is used during the ML model training process. In other words, the primary goal of model training is to minimise the loss function by adjusting model parameters. A good loss function helps strike a balance between model underfitting and overfitting. Loss functions in regression training are Mean Squared Error (MSE), Root Mean Squared Error (RMSE), Mean Absolute Error (MAE), and Mean Absolute Percentage Error (MAPE). Examples of regression model training processes are linear regression, polynomial regression, gradient boosting regression, regression decision trees, regression random forests, and neural network regression.

Classification loss functions are Binary Cross-Entropy for binary classification problems, Categorical Cross-Entropy for multi-class classification, and Hinge loss for Support Vector Machines (SVM). Popular classification model training processes are logistic regression, classification decision trees, classification random forests, SVM, K-nearest neighbours and neural network classification. Loss functions not only help us determine the best equation representing our model but also help us compare across various models.

interview topics in statistics for ML

- → empirical data
- → descriptive statistics (factual)
- → central tendency (mean / median / mode)
- → dispersion (variance / SD)
- → distribution of data
- → inferential statistics (uncertainty)
- → central limit theorem in ML
- → hypothesis testing
- → parametric vs. non parametric tests
- → loss functions
- → regression
  - → MSE
  - → RMSE
  - → MAE
  - → MAPE
  - → classification
    - → binary cross entropy
    - → categorical cross entropy
    - → hinge loss

SECTION D

THE REVOLUTION:
GEN AI BEST PRACTICES

Siddharth to Varun: Just as I felt I had mastered the data science field, a paradigm shift occurred - the rise of Generative AI. The seventeen articles in this section become chapters in my journey of discovery while exploring this new frontier, marvelling at its potential, and rapidly adapting the necessary skills.

MAKING LARGE LANGUAGE MODELS RELEVANT TO AN ORGANIZATION

If data were alcohol, I am drunk. Forever. Providing a Generative AI based chatbot for an organization is the second step. The first step in applying Generative AI for business benefits is to declutter the space of Generative AI and have a strategic roadmap for the next couple of years. A shorter roadmap is not a lack of vision. Instead, it respects the speed of technological development taking place around us in the field of Generative AI. People often confuse between "Generative AI (GenAI)" and "General AI (Artificial General Intelligence or AGI)". GenAI is not yet AGI, even though it might be one step closer to AGI. Large Language Models (LLMs) are the foundation models. I am glad they are called so. I am not going to write about GenAI strategy design. However, I plan to throw light on something that will help you understand a GenAI strategy and enable you to ask the right questions.

LLMs are built using the revolutionary transformer architecture. While the applications of LLMs are limitless, the world has started using them extensively for information extraction, text summarization, question answering, code generation, text classification (sentiment and topic analysis), virtual assistants, source codes and error explanation, and a host of other natural language processing use cases. One example of such a use case is a voice assistant designed using an LLM. The dataset changes hands in the following manner (human speech → text → context → prompt → LLM → text → machine speech).

Prompt engineering is the art and science of communicating with a Generative AI tool (LLM). An LLM is good at open ended language generation which might not be useful directly as it is for many of our needs. It requires guidance. A skilfully engineered prompt provides that guidance to the LLM. Structurally, the prompt should contain the instruction specifying the primary intent (example -summarize text), the context (example – dialogue between a data scientist and business user) and the constraints within which the LLM should respond (example – in less than 10 lines, in PDF format). LLM based application building frameworks often take parameters to ensure that the most desired response is received from the LLM. LLM itself takes parameters such as the "temperature". A high temperature value returns a diverse response which could be more probabilistic and creative. Similarly, a low temperature value might make the output more deterministic. Different LLMs might have the temperature parameter influencing different attributes of the output generated. They might have different temperature ranges as well.

If dealing with textual prompts sounds difficult, now we have multimodal prompts including text, image, audio and video. The beauty of prompt engineering is that it enables non-technical users too to interact with LLMs. An efficient LLM based application building framework such as LangChain makes using multiple LLMs possible, using same LLM multiple times possible, solves to some extent the short-term memory issue of LLMs because of the limit on the number of tokens, and helps integrate LLMs into data pipelines.

Here goes my personal opinion. Feel free to disagree. I have seen LLMs quite creative in writing a poem, a story, summarizing a paragraph, language translation and many other general-purpose tasks. I don't mind using them for such tasks. However, when we provide an LLM based chatbot solution to a consumer processed goods (CPG) organization for example, we should do the following. 1) Train a customized CPG_LLM with historical conversations using one of the general-purpose pretrained LLMs 2) Use an LLM based application building framework such as LangChain to provide the prompt to CPG_LLM and format the response from CPG_LLM 3) Marry the CPG_LLM response with other relevant structured information available with the organization 4) Display the final output to the chatbot user.

Doing this will ensure that our chatbot is intelligent and responds to the user, based on relevant numbers and not only with a creativity of language generation. Guess what. Since, we have trained our CPG_LLM with conversations from this particular organization, we would expect the chatbot to retain the flavour of the industry, the flavour of the organization and the flavour of the department the chatbot is deployed in. What I mean to say is, a solution based on training an LLM with additional relevant data, based on prompt engineered interfacing, and based on business logic treated output, is far more relevant and effective for an organization than a solution simply relying on scarcely treated LLMs. Because LLMs are trained on super huge volumes of language data, they appear to have the "common sense" of a human being. I have definitely got myself wiser while writing this piece. I hope you too, while reading.

transformer architecture
prompt engineering
    ↳ instruction
    ↳ context
    ↳ constraints
temperature as a parameter
contextualising LLMs
    ↳ fine tuning the LLM
    ↳ RAG
LLMs appear to have common sense

LOVE-STRUCK

"*Saw your smile with admiration / Saw your dress with love / Heard your words with attention / Heard your thoughts with care / Never could I say I liked you / Never could I say I loved you / Never could I give a flower / Never could I climb a tower / To show how much I loved / To show how much I loved*"

If LLM were a person, I would have loved them. Deeply. Irrespective of whether it was a 'him' or a 'her'. A few weeks ago, someone I chatted with for the first time was mindful enough to check if I could bring my partner along for lunch. Calling the partner a partner was a considerate mannerism. Stayed clear of any misassumptions. Let's call LLM a partner.

Among all the other things that need to be taken care of, one has to keep track of the costs incurred from hitting the LLM multiple times. One can do that by capturing the number of tokens passed to and received from the LLM. Usually, LLM API providers charge based on the total number of tokens over a period of time. Hence, optimised ways of interacting with LLMs come into play. You will be punished for mindlessly loading the LLM with records and records of datasets, and paragraphs of instructions in the prompt. Others and Google searches tell me cost calculation, and optimisation are not featured in most prompt engineering courses. Lately, I have been experimenting with Generative AI quite a bit as part of my work. I have realised that a good prompt should do the following: 1) Get you a precise and required response, 2) Get you a response in a structure that is easily consumable, and 3) Not cost you a fortune.

Certain practices would help in controlling your costs. First, measure the tokens exchanged. The first step to improving something is to measure it. You can create a simple functionality for tracking the count of tokens for an individual, a use case, a team, and an organisation. Second, avoid hitting the LLM when you can. For example, if the variable you are trying to investigate gets populated before the LLM call, you should use a function similar to 'exit()' before the LLM is triggered. Third, employ a stub as the LLM response. For example, one has to work extensively on the UI (User Interface) with a minor change in colour or placement of an image each time. Use the dummy output from the LLM for such experiments instead of hitting the LLM each time.

There are a few more ways of dealing with LLMs smartly. I will discuss them after I become wiser in the coming days. Generative AI is here to help us in myriad use cases in every domain, including healthcare, manufacturing, retail, finance, telecom, banking, media, insurance, and the rest. It solves the requirements of creative content creation, document summarisation, data interpretation, etc. The only thing left of coding is understanding the requirements (both business and technical) and articulating the context correctly. With Generative AI, everyone is a programmer, similar to what the NVIDIA chief said a few months ago.

As it is said, ignorantia juris non excusat (not knowing the law is not an excuse). With the risk of stretching it too far, I can say the same about Generative AI today. A salesperson or a marketing specialist must know how Generative AI can enhance an organisation's sales or marketing functions. They should be aware of how it makes their work simpler, more creative and consequently more effective. The call centre should appreciate how Generative AI can be used through an internal intelligent chatbot to help understand customers' pain points, interpret data points, view customers' journeys so far with the organisation, and recommend ways of dealing with the customer while having the conversation. There is a high chance that this will lead to a meaningful conversation culminating in a smooth customer experience. My best wishes to all of you for more exciting Generative times while I continue my romance with the LLMs.

counting tokens to and from the LLM
good prompt
 ↳ gives precise response
 ↳ in a consumable structure
 ↳ not cost a fortune
best practices
 ↳ measure tokens
 ↳ preemptively exit wherever possible
 ↳ use stuff as LLM response

THE RAG-ING SUCCESS OF LLMS

I have always said that the space between a human and an LLM is made up of prompt engineering. Through this article today, let me admit that the space is actually made up of prompt engineering and RAG. We have seen the flurry of experiments and activities that the advent of LLMs has brought us. LLMs (Large Language Models) are the foundational models. They are rewriting the narrative of how we work and live.

Not many build them from scratch because building one requires humongous storage, processing power, time, and money. It takes almost one "internet" as its input dataset. The input dataset contains part of a sentence as the feature variable set and the immediately following word (or token) as the target variable. However, if this data was prepared while India was celebrating its Independence Day last year, the foundational LLM model misses any new knowledge over the past half year. Hence, there is a cut-off date of knowledge for each LLM. As users of the LLM, we should know what that cut-off date is. When humans attempt to answer a question they are unsure of, they show hesitation through their voice or body language. This is not the same with LLMs. They "lie with confidence" when they are unsure of the answer. Dangerous, right? Somebody, please teach them effective body language!

LLM creators have always advised you to fine-tune the LLM with additional data relevant to the purpose of your usage. This is called "Supervised Fine-Tuning". It's not an easy job, requiring substantial time, money, and processing power. In addition, supervised fine-tuning causes the parametric weights and, hence, the inherent nature of the foundational LLM to change. We expect it to change towards our specific requirement and not away from it. So, additional evaluations must be carried out to ensure the LLM works as an LLM. Having said this, I am mindful that there is PEFT (Parameter Efficient Fine Tuning), where a small number of parameters will be updated, as opposed to the full LLM fine-tuning, where all the model parameters are updated.

RAG (Retrieval Augmented Generation) comes to the rescue here. In simple terms, we AUGMENT the prompt (the question the user asks the LLM) by RETRIEVING additional information from our local database before asking the LLM to GENERATE the response. In other words, we provide additional context to the LLM without touching its foundational structure. Simple, effective, and economical. It could be a local database or any other internal or external knowledge source for efficient search and retrieval. RAG brings in additional context, reduces hallucinations (lying with confidence), and does not disturb the foundational properties of the base LLM. Storing and retrieving matching contextual information from the local database is a complete area of study. The match is between which two things here? It is between the prompt that the user types and the data or documents stored in the local database. Unsurprisingly, we want to match and evaluate again after the LLM responds. In case of deviations from the expectation, revise the storage, retrieval, or augmenting technique. The match is now among which three things? It is among the responses from the LLM, information stored in the local database, and our requirements for using an LLM in the first place. Evaluation of RAG-enabled LLM responses is another area of study by itself.

How many areas of study have I mentioned in this article? Prompt engineering, RAG storage, RAG retrieval, and LLM response evaluation. And I am talking only about LLM usage. Leave aside building foundational LLM models using transformers. In addition, there are unimodal and multimodal data exchanges across the three entities (the user, the RAG knowledge source, and the LLM). The content types could be text, image, audio, and video. Unimodal consists of any one type of the four. Multimodal means the combination of at least two of the four types. For example, we are looking at a multimodal prompt, a multimodal data storage in the RAG knowledge source, a multimodal matching, a multimodal retrieval, a multimodal prompt augmentation, a multimodal LLM response, and a multimodal response evaluation.

base vs. foundational LLMs

LLMs predict next word

cut offs date of knowledge

hallucinations

supervised fine tuning of LLMs

PEFT (parameter efficient fine tuning)

RAG
    ↳ Retrieve context
    ↳ Augment prompt
    ↳ generate response
    ↳ reduces hallucinations
    ↳ RAG knowledge source
    ↳ multimodal RAG

THE DOPAMINE IN LLMS

"**M**an is a social animal" was our one-size-fits-all essay opening sentence. If the essay was on "The Cow", we began with "Man is a social animal. Cows are not. A cow has four legs…". If the topic was "The Cricket Match", we started with "Man is a social animal. They play cricket. A cricket team …". You get the trick which helped children hit the ground running in examinations. Today, my topic is "The Large Language Models".

Man is a social animal. The dopamine in their brain gives the thrill of expectation, desire, and creativity. It fires the quest for more even after having all the world's money, friends, and pleasure. If somebody said Open AI was behind the LLM revolution, let us be biologically correct. It was the dopamine. Most likely Sam's. Speaking of LLMs, can generative AI help us create synthetic customers? I found more questions than answers in my debates with colleagues over the last few weeks. The considerations are: 1) What do we want to use the synthetic customers for? 2) What is the profile of a synthetic customer? In other words, which set of variables you must use for defining your customer precisely and completely? 3) Can a synthetic customer replace a real customer? Akin to asking whether AI can replace human beings. 4) Are LLMs placed well to generate not only a creative poem but also a quantitatively meaningful entity?

Provide a quantitative skeleton to your LLM generation. One can use RAG (Retrieval Augmented Generation) to retrieve additional information from knowledge sources, provide numeric constraints in the prompt, or use third-party non-LLM tools known more for quantitative precision than for understanding the natural language. LLMs can decide to extract the numbers from another tool based on the user query and package and display it to continue conversing with the human. One such quantitative skeleton could be helpful in reverse sentiment analysis. I could ask the LLM to generate a customer comment with a sentiment score of 3/10, where a score of more than 5 denotes positive sentiment. In contrast, a score from 0 to 5 (including the boundaries) indicates negative sentiment. I could ask all negative sentiment instances in the comment to be clustered in the second half. The generated comment has to align with the customer's profile (the synthetic customer, I mean). If the synthetic customer has 80% of his calls to the call centre as repeat calls for the issue with the highest frequency of occurrence in his kitty, the LLM must generate the comment accordingly. I just described a quantitative skeleton I was referring to earlier. The dopamine level in an LLM is controlled by a parameter called "temperature".

Defining the profile of a synthetic customer is critical. Ideally, it should match the profile of your real customer. Instead, I should say it should match the profile of the real customer you have stored in your database. This is because you are going to create synthetic customers from real customers. I am mindful of the argument that we are talking about taking the real customer out of the picture, which is impermissible. I recommend augmenting instead of replacing and non-intrusive instead of meddlesome.

In this article, I have mentioned three first-time phrases: 1) Quantitative skeleton, 2) Reverse sentiment analysis, and 3) Sentiment instances within a customer comment. However, feel free to disagree with my thoughts on the efficacy of synthetic customers. I have always believed that an agreement helps the ego while a disagreement helps innovation. Let's innovate. While you complete reading this, I will recharge my dopamine levels.

FLY HIGH BECAUSE THE SKY IS FORGIVING

The deep tech vs. consumer tech debate is quite hot among Indians today. This is a good debate regarding where India stands today in the generative AI space. Have we missed the bus in developing our own foundational LLM? Are we good at only using LLMs that others have created? Is India seen only as a consumer of AI and not so much as a producer of AI? Do we still have a chance to win the race? I do not have complete answers to all these questions, probably any of them. At the same time, I will not write India off the Generative AI map.

Foundational LLMs require building models from scratch by collecting training data from various online sources. They do not use any pre-trained models as their starting point. The rise of Indic LLMs is noteworthy. If I am not wrong, BharatGPT covers 14 Indian languages for voice and 22 for text. It handles a wide range of natural language (NL) processing tasks. We can have data sovereignty. Data stays within the boundaries of India. It is tailored for Indian users by retaining the cultural context and language nuances. A similar story and capabilities go for Krutrim. The Bhashini ecosystem aims to collect multilingual data and build Generative AI products in Indian languages while dissolving linguistic barriers nationwide. OpenHathi from Sarvam AI is contributing to the Indian AI ecosystem and encouraging innovation in LLMs.

We need deep pockets to invest in AI research. It boils down to a quick short-term monetisation vs. a long-term ROI (Return on Investment) mindset. The difference is whether the workforce is working on the theory of AI or its applications. How many Indians are working on building the next revolutionary AI algorithm that will change the rules of the game? There must be a balance between foundational research and profitable applications of LLMs. The balance will ensure that Generative AI efforts are sustainable while not undermining the need for long-term research funding.

Not every use case would require the complete foundational capabilities of existing LLMs. On the lines of building LLMs from scratch, let me propose to train a "life model", which shall predict what event will happen next in my life given the knowledge of the sequence of events that have taken place in my life till today. For the labelled data, let us pick all those sequences of events that have taken place in people's lives from sources such as digital biography books, online articles on individuals, including the famous and the infamous, and Wikipedia pages talking about people. For this purpose, filtering and creating the life model training data of event sequences from the training dataset used for foundational LLMs is not bad. We will have to define the "vocabulary", which should be the set of all possible life events that have ever occurred. That would mean we must decide on the granularity of life events as per our model. The granularity level should be determined by what level of life events we readily have available with us and what level we want to predict someone's next life event. One difference I see between words (tokens) and life events (also tokens) is that the "vocabulary" of life events might be relatively smaller compared to the vocabulary of the English language. Does that mean we can create training samples manually by studying lives? Can I then explicitly use the life model to state how my day will look like tomorrow?

Can we then understand the pattern of successful lives? Of course, we must determine what success means to different individuals (financial, social, personal, professional, and all-around). Can someone then know what future steps would lead to their aspired position in a profession or society? I am trying to say that this is an example of a use case where we start building our LLM from scratch. The linguistic generative power of a pre-trained foundational LLM will not be required here.

The curtains are not down yet, and they probably will never be. The play will be on as long as we can come up with the next big thing. With one-sixth of the world's brain tissues, India cannot be ignored from the Generative AI map.

WASHING OFF THE KALANK

"Papa lun, Papa lun, fast fast lun," my son screams excitedly while riding the balance cycle. Balance cycles are the ones without pedals or support wheels. You ride them, pushing with your legs, and learn to balance before you learn cycling. I keep running behind to stop him from falling and save him from the scooter and car drivers (More precisely, to save the drivers from him!). He does not get tired. We switch to playing football. A balloon-weight football. It only goes so far when he kicks. It does not get far either when I kick. Within five minutes of trying to tame the ball, he gives up. "Papa lun, Papa lun, fast fast lun". We are back with the balance cycle.

True. It is hard to do difficult things. Did you not notice the adjective? Two weeks ago, I wrote about concerns with LLMs learning from our non-idealistic past. Raising concerns is easy. Providing solutions is hard. Today, I am going to try the hard part.

First, select only unbiased content to prepare the training data set. Apply the filter right at the outset. The approach gels well with reason. Let's not learn from the bad guys. However, there is a problem. LLMs' language comprehension and generation capabilities are reduced with fewer training records. If input data is restricted, at some point, we are effectively converting the LLM into an SLM (Small Language Model). One way to work around this is not to remove the biased content. Instead, existing LLMs can be used to convert biased data into synthetic unbiased data and then pass on the unbiased data as part of the training dataset. We don't lose records. Then, our LLMs will live a godly life.

Second, biased content can be stored as vectors in a vector database. Vectors are numeric avatars of words. They magically enable us to store the relationships among words and the context. In a technique such as RAG (Retrieval Augmented Generation), we use this repository to augment the prompt passed to the LLM by contextualizing it. In our case, I should probably call it the "Repository of Kalank", which would provide the "anti-context". Topics or relationships like the ones stored in that database should be avoided. Effectively, we can "sanitize" the prompt before passing it to the LLM. What more? We can "sanitize" the response from the LLM as well before displaying it to the user. As a good practice, keep updating the database as we encounter more avoidable biases.

Third, humans should practice responsible prompting. Instead of blaming the LLM for generating content that reflects gender, social, economic, geographical, or racial discrimination, why not explicitly request the LLM through our prompts to avoid such biases? Having understood the technology that has created them, I am sure the LLM will oblige. Moreover, if we don't want to leave it to the user, let the LLM provider have fixed instructions to append to any prompt asking the LLM to behave well. The challenge is that users will be left with a reduced context window. Context window is the sum of words passed to the LLM plus those received from the LLM. Context window is a technical constraint of the neural network.

Fourth, emphasize the crucial role of humans-in-the-loop (HITL) in creating LLMs, using them, and making business decisions based on their recommendations. This is not just about having humans-in-the-loop, but about having "good-humans-in-the-loop" (GHITL) who are valued for their ethical judgment and oversight.

Fifth, let us be clear on what we want. The internet is a mirror we are staring at. We have created volumes and volumes of maligned content. It reflects who we are. Do we want LLMs to reflect reality or to be idealistic? Are they the real LLMs or the ideal LLMs that will take us towards AGI (Artificial General Intelligence)? Do we want LLMs to be us? If not, then we have a problem. We don't want us. Why fix LLMs? Fix us. Behave no evil, speak no evil, write no evil, create no evil, and post no evil. The LLM that will be born ten years hence will look at their training dataset and marvel at humans' wonderful society. It will marvel at what a wonderful LLM it will become!

"Papa lun, Papa Lun", he asserts again, riding his balance cycle. He is doing his easier bit. I will do my easier bit. Let me go and list down the concerns I have against him and leave the solving part to you!

how to build a well behaved LLM ?

    ⤷ include only unbiased data in train set

    ⤷ anti context provided by repository of kalank

    ⤷ responsible prompting

    ⤷ human in the loop

    ⤷ decide whether we want reality or idealism

TIME, TIDE, AND TOKENS WAIT FOR NONE

I wake up. It is 7 am this Monday. I am panicking. Friday is not the day of celebrations. It is the day of celebrations and over-commitments. In fluent spoken English, I had promised to deliver the world by Monday evening. By world, I mean a set of efficient prompts and consumable LLM responses. Talk about my learning from mistakes! The total cost of the weekend drive to Bangalore looked like diesel prices, toll charges, and excuses. My son wakes up. He spends five minutes of settling-down time. When I was about to start my work for the day, he jumped up and screamed, "Papa, dance." Alexa played "Uthe Sabke Kadam Dekho Ram Pam Pam" from the Bollywood movie Baton Baton Mein. I force-obliged. I have a video of the dance. I follow his dance steps. The only difference is he looks cute. Little did he know that time was money for me. Or should I say, "Token was money?"

In the LLMs, the maximum sequence length a transformer can process at a time is called the context window. This is defined at the time of training the model. This length is the number of tokens, not words. A token is a unit the LLM deals with and could be a sub-word, space or punctuation mark. Therefore, the NLP process always starts with a "tokeniser". It is easier for the LLM to understand human language through tokens and not words. My immediate question is, why don't we speak and write in tokens? That is for another day. In practice, the number of words is approximately three-fourths of the number of tokens.

Given the LLM's limitation in processing only a specific number of tokens at a time, strategies like RAG have gained significant traction. RAG, in essence, strives to maximise the context within the prompt while minimising the number of tokens used. This approach highlights the importance of token management. On the other hand, expanding the context window comes at a high cost. If the length of an input sequence triples, the memory requirement increases ninefold. For instance, with a context window increase from 4k to 16k, the memory requirement skyrockets to 16 times the original.

The idea is for the context window to contain the complete essence of the communication in the tokens. Hence, we store the token's position as well. Such positional encoding is achieved by storing the token's absolute or relative position. We discuss deciding on the context window size while training an LLM from scratch. However, there are approaches for increasing the context window of pre-trained models.

With the risk of infusing boredom into you, I would like to repeat what I had said three months ago. Or, in software parlance, I can be happy that I produced something reusable three months ago. Most LLM providers charge per token. Certain practices would help in controlling your costs. First, measure the tokens exchanged. The first step to improving something is to measure it. You can create a simple functionality for tracking the count of tokens for an individual, an application, a team, and an organisation. Second, avoid hitting the LLM when you can. For example, if the variable you are trying to investigate gets populated before the LLM call, you should use a function like 'exit' before the LLM is triggered. Third, employ a stub as the LLM response when one must work extensively on the UI (User Interface) with a minor change in colour or placement of a button each time. Use the dummy output from the LLM for such experiments instead of hitting the LLM each time. Fourth, as mentioned above, use RAG (Retrieval Augmented Generation).

Now, while my son is dancing his morning away (alone), I am working on the best token management approach. Alexa is playing *"Nadiya chale chale re dhara / Chanda chale chale re taara / Tujhko chalna hoga, tujhko chalna hoga."*

context window defined before model training
tokens ae units of LLM interaction
RAG
token management
longer context window needs more memory
longer context window increases chances of hallucinations
positional encoding
controlling token costs

WHEN INSTALLING PACKAGES TOOK LONGER THAN CODING

This week, I experimented with building a CNN (Convolutional Neural Network) image classification model. I wanted to give GitHub Copilot a try. GitHub Copilot is an AI pair programmer that helps with code completions. One can ask the tool to "explain" a segment of code, fix an error, or generate a Python docstring. Python docstring is a sentence documenting what the module, class, or method does.

Before I started coding, installing the required Python packages took me about forty minutes. The actual coding consisted of fifty lines of code and took less than ten minutes. A few things stood out.

I got comment-completion recommendations from the editor when I started typing. The recommendations were not without substance. For example, after the block of code that fits the CNN model, the suggestion was to evaluate and then save the model. This might be a simple suggestion for experienced data scientists. However, think about someone learning to build an ML model for the first time. This is non-trivial.

Immediately after I accepted the tool's suggestion to complete the comment line, it suggested the content of the whole function. That was another nine lines of code. It intelligently picked up the function name, variable names, keywords, and parameters. Only the parameter values were out of place for obvious reasons. The tool did not have details of the input images, which were placed in my system's local directory. However, it was easy to change the values given that I already had the syntactically correct function written by the tool.

It did well when I asked the Copilot to explain a selected part of the code. I was presented with conceptual details of keywords contained in the selected part. It was interesting to note that the text was not a static piece of content as opposed to what one may assume. The explanation was in context to my program. It highlighted details of what should come next because I had ended my selection abruptly in the middle of a line of code.

What made me feel that the tool "understands" Python code was its ability to generate a couple of lines of text (called a docstring in coding parlance) explaining the complete source code, a class, and a method. It was human-like, I would say.

That was not all. I needed to do some documentation for the model I had built. Guess what? After having all the commented lines inside the program, the docstrings, and the conceptual explanation of the keywords, I finished the documentation in a jiffy.

While excited at this newfound superpower, I am mindful of its shortcomings. I am not talking about inaccurate suggestions from the tool. I am talking about the practice. What did I miss by spending less than ten minutes writing my code? I missed another twenty ways of not coding. I missed the red error highlights, the browsing and skimming through stacks of web pages, the Stack Overflow banter, the confidence that "I got you" this time, and the dashing of that confidence. And I missed repeating the above cycle multiple times. Is this not how I learned programming till now?

The increase in productivity comes at a price (other than the monthly subscription fees of GitHub Copilot). I am talking about GitHub Copilot here. However, it could be any of the plethora of AI programming tools available today. The increase in productivity leads organisations to contemplate reducing the size of their programming teams. If done hastily, the move might backfire. After all, only a good programmer recognises another good programmer. Changing the parameter values mentioned above while defining the CNN model is critical to meeting the program objectives. We got a "working" model swiftly and saved a ton of coding and documentation time. While we finalise whether the advantages of such a tool supersede the disadvantages, allow me to bask in the excitement of the future of programming (and content generation).

GENERATIVE AI PRESENTATION FOR BEGINNERS (45 MINUTES)

This column did not post an article last week for the first time since 15 November last year. I would have loved a no-week-missed year and was working towards that. I was glad to watch kid's videos with my son that teach how it is quite possible for things to go against the plan. I love the 2019 Bollywood movie Chhichhore, in which Anni tries to throw the ball into the basketball goal, but it bounces back from the hoop. They lose the match. H3 Hostel won the game. But they cheered H4 Hostel for their team spirit and perseverance. A less than perfect ending. Quite frequent and relatable. On lines like the above, I might not be able to give you the best (or the only) outline for a 45-minute presentation on Generative AI. You decide.

First, The Generative AI Revolution. If the Generative AI hype is based on truth, is it still hype? Talk about my convoluted thoughts. Generative AI generates content in the form of text, audio, music, images, and videos. It has applications in every function and every industry. The impact is in how we work, write our job descriptions and the expectations from a role in an organisation. There is a myriad of use cases to explore. The list of use cases is limited only by our imagination.

Second, Insights into the Creation of the Training Dataset. The training dataset for building an LLM is created by taking each word of a part of the sentence as an input variable and the subsequent word as the output variable. The model generates by predicting the next word. In a standard multiclass classification ML problem, the word with the highest probability of occurrence should be picked. However, selecting the topmost word every time would cause the loss of creativity of LLMs. Hence, quite often, we go further down.

Third, Is Gen AI Supervised Learning? Taking the online content as input and generating the LLM's output makes it an unsupervised model. However, as we look deeper, we see that the actual LLM is created as a supervised model, as explained in the above section.

Fourth, Three Ways of Using an LLM. We can use a foundational LLM as it is, fine-tune it to create our domain-specific LLM or use RAG with a foundational LLM to contextualise the response. The second and third approaches can also be used in combination.

Fifth, LLM-based Application. The application we build using LLMs generally leverages the natural language understanding and generation capabilities of the LLMs. There are configuration files storing details of the LLM and its parameters. It would also require creating the most effective prompt (prompt engineering) and parsing the response into a consumable format. The application would often use agents and third-party tools to carry out specialised tasks requested by the user.

Sixth, Challenges with LLMs. Working with LLMs is not a bed of roses. Challenges include hallucinations, a lack of computation capability, inaccurate answers to fact-based questions, a cut-off date of knowledge, token limits, inaccurate code generation, a threat to data privacy and intellectual property ownership, a threat to ethics, job losses, and a lack of talent available to work with LLMs, to name a few.

Seventh, Best Practices for Developing with LLMs. The developer must incorporate effective prompting techniques that will help get the most contextual response in the most consumable format with an optimised number of tokens. One must optimise the number of calls made to the LLM during experimentation by using stubs and drivers. The design of the application should not enforce unnecessary usage of the LLM. The trade-off between getting an LLM to do a task and writing a piece of code to do the task should be respected.

Eighth, A Learning Pathway. The fundamentals of supervised and unsupervised learning in ML hold good for LLMs. The fundamentals of statistics matter as well. One cannot be on the tenth step by starting on the tenth. The journey must cover deep learning through artificial neural networks. Fluency with data, vector databases, and data exploration go a long way in making the trip exciting and possible.

Now, let's move on to the Q&A. We have 15 minutes left. Who goes first?

Gen AI Presentation
- Gen AI revolution
- creating training dataset
- supervised or unsupervised?
- 3 ways of using an LLM
- LLM based app architecture
- challenges
- best practices for developing LLM based apps
- a learning pathway

A MULTI-AGENT WORLD

A team achieves more than an individual can do. One team member might be good at generating ideas, another at expanding the ideas to a plot, another at finding inaccuracies and editing the content, and yet another at designing the content to make it look readable and attractive. Each of them is an individual with a specific specialised skill. One consumable product is developed when they all come together as a team.

Using a multi-agent framework to build LLM-powered applications is not very different. We can consider each agent an individual in the content creation team mentioned above. We assign each agent a role, goal, and background story (a context). In our case, the roles would be idea generator, creative writer, editor, and content designer. Agents must interact and collaborate with other agents for the final product to succeed. What use is highly readable and attractive content when the plot is uninteresting?

Here is what I am getting to. Each of us is an agent in the larger team. I am not focusing on one specialised skill of an individual. An individual never uses the skill isolated. Instead, the whole package (the individual) does the task. All attributes, such as attitude, soft skills, outlook, mood, aptitude, learnability and presence of mind, are at play while applying a skill to the task.

What if there is a way to describe (or list out) my personality in totality? That would include my demeanour, likes, dislikes, comfort zones, temperament, and whatnot. It is like merging my Facebook, LinkedIn, Twitter, and Instagram profiles. There is no harm in taking a few activities from the platforms as sample behaviour. Multiply that many thousand times. Is that an agent having my personality? Can it mimic my thought process, behaviour in situations, decision-making, talent, IQ and EQ levels, writing and speaking styles? I know. We also thought feeding all online content as a training dataset to an algorithm to build an ML model sounded impossible until it was done. And you see what it is doing to the world. Considering the agent as a complete package is critical here. I come with my baggage and background story.

Your agentic replicas could be used in many cases. Imagine my CTO is unavailable for a meeting to discuss my new idea for building the next LLM-powered application. Can I have the meeting with his agent instead? It is not difficult to determine if the agentic CTO is doing equally well as the CTO. In the meeting, nearly ten people would interact and share ideas and feedback with the agentic CTO. Of course, the set of agents I have access to (akin to LinkedIn connections or Facebook friends) and how I use the data securely is something to be designed.

More questions arise. Who is responsible for an agent's decisions? Once an agent is created, how do we keep it updated with the new skills that one individual gains? How do we provide the context of events a day ago? Or 10 minutes ago?

Once an agent has made suggestions, how do we ensure it remembers what it said earlier? How do we ensure the agent never crosses the boundaries of social, personal, and professional behaviour? How do you define the geographical boundaries of agents? Does this mean the world will be a multi-agent system, with India having 140 crore agents and the world having 8 billion? They play their roles, have their goals, have their backstories, execute their tasks, and live their lives. They are a team set out to make the world the happiest place. Will I be available in my agentic form after I die? If yes, who gets to control it?

I have an Adhaar number, and many of you have an SSN (Social Security Number). Wait until I give you my Agent Identification Number (AIN). Or the AIN of my CTO!

SHOOT-AT-SIGHT ORDER ISSUED AGAINST THE BUG

I have been ecstatic about AI Pair Programming over the past few months and am experiencing its benefits firsthand. However, taking a step back, I ask who the real beneficiary is from the magical programming powers. The coder? He completes coding without having to go through countless experimental errors while developing. This increases the ease of development and, hence, confidence. You tell me later whether it is helping the coder in the long run. The employer? He enjoys increased productivity. More software products and services can be delivered within a shorter period. The employer benefits hugely if the customer pays based on products or features, not effort. The customer? If effort-saving benefits are passed on to the customer, they will spend less for the same product and service compared to pre-generative AI days. I know you will hate me if I say humanity benefits.

I wanted to return to AI Pair Programming in the coder's scenario. Twenty years ago, if I were asked whether a specific application or functionality could be developed, I would have explored it before confirming. These days, I say, "Yes, it can be done", and then research how to do it. No coding technique is beyond our reach because of the many valuable resources (including LLMs that generate codes) available. This is true whether or not you have experience programming in the required language. This has made the programming skill language agnostic. It's a fantastic scenario, I would say.

LLM's creativity sometimes gets the coder in trouble, especially when the LLM is not asked the question in the best way. Everyone is a prompt engineer these days. You ask, get a response, see the gap, revise the prompt, ask again, and get the desired response. Creating an LLM-based application is not data science. Creating an LLM from scratch or fine-tuning a foundational LLM is data science because it involves getting an ML model as output at the end of the exercise. Creating an LLM-based application is like using a churn-prediction model built a year ago by someone else to predict customer X's likely churn in the next three months. Of course, you are also building the functionality allowing the user to consume the model's prediction. As I have always said, a good data scientist is not one who builds good models.

Instead, he is one who builds good models that solve business problems.

There is one more troubling trend I foresee. As the level of abstraction increases for the regular programmer, the size of the black box increases. When we have waded through "silly" errors for hours, we have learnt. We have learnt concepts of programming. We have learnt how not to code. For someone with such a background, it might be easy to approve or disapprove of the bot's recommendation for the following five lines of code. Ten years hence, how strong will the human in the "human in the loop (HITL)" programming be? This necessitates that the LLM start generating high-quality code recommendations, maintaining a high standard of explainability.

In the debate of whether AI has intelligence (despite "I" standing for "Intelligence"), I vote for the negative as of today. However, I look forward to transitioning from human programming to AI pair programming to AI-only programming. We will achieve AI-only programming when the HITL does nothing but press the TAB and ENTER keys on the keyboard. With agents and tools providing the support necessary for LLMs to manage, coordinate, execute, and delegate work while mimicking skilled individuals or resourceful organisations, we might not be too far from AI-only programming. GitHub Copilot (powered by Open AI's Codex), Amazon CodeWhisperer, Mistral AI's Codestral, and AlphaCode by DeepMind have already given us a competitive advantage. Who are we competing against? Ourselves. Enough of the leading by example (henceforth deemed preaching by example). Let me get back to the coding before AI takes it away!

THE WEEKEND GETAWAY WITH LLMS

The topic of weekend getaways has become popular among those working hard or pretending to do so during the weekdays. We are getting away from what? I am inclined to offer, "from life". I did ask the Llama 3.1 8B LLM running locally on my computer a few related questions. It promptly answered, "Pondicherry (2 hours from Chennai), Tiruvannamalai (3 hours from Chennai), Kanchipuram (4 hours from Chennai), Mahabalipuram (1 hour from Chennai), and Vellore (2.5 hours from Chennai)."

I turned philosophical and asked, "What are the top places for a weekend getaway from life?". The model answered with a list of places. "What are the top places for breaking free from life?". A list of places came again. "What are the top places for a weekend getaway from living?" Another list featured. "What are the places near life?" It answered, "Venus, Mars, and Moon." I started losing patience and typed hard as if it were life or death for me. But it was about life AND death. My life and my death! "Considering that you are philosophical by nature, what are the weekend getaways from life?". The answer had an unimpressive list of parks, greenery, and beaches around Chennai. Why would not a philosopher be at a beach over the weekend? Fair enough. "What can I do other than live life? What is there before and after life?" Finally, it answered the closest I expected. "Pre-life has not yet been discovered scientifically, and the concept of the afterlife varies among different cultures and religions." Phew!

The foundational LLM has a broad knowledge of everything. It is like a jack of all trades and master of none. The LLM needs to know which role they are playing. We should assign them a personality and skill set and tell them their likes and dislikes. This is where agents help. In addition, it makes designing the prompt easy, customisable and modularised for each agent.

The other way to specialise in an area is to retrain (supervised fine-tuning) the LLM with data only from the desired area of expertise. Ask the general physician LLM about your health, the astrologer LLM about your future, the math LLM to compute, and the climate LLM about ecological disruptions due to an increase in the earth's temperature. Imagine the computing resources you need to retrain the four LLMs to impart the specialisation. In addition, imagine the hardware you would need to run all four specialised LLMs (or experts) in your local system so that they respond with coherence. We find the approach with one LLM and four agents simpler.

In a multi-agent ecosystem, the LLM precisely plays the role of each agent as necessary. Many multi-agent creation frameworks, including AutoGen, CrewAI, and LangGraph, are already available. The LLM also plays the orchestrator or coordinator who decides which agent to invoke when. The output of one agent goes as input for the subsequent one. This is a powerful concept of teamwork.

The sweet spot with 32 GB RAM and 8 GB vRAM consumer hardware is a four-bit quantised LLM with 8 billion parameters. Quantisation is a compression technique that reduces the model's hunger for memory. Given current levels of human patience, inferencing occurs at an acceptable speed. Those suffering from patience malnutrition go with a 16 GB vRAM. It is essential to state that patience malnutrition causes financial malnutrition, leading to calorie malnutrition. Compression techniques enable us to run the LLM locally in the first place. However, accuracy is not their greatest fan.

You can create a service around the LLM, build a simple UI, and expose it to the world, which is tens and tens of friends in the case of socially malnutritioned people like me.

getting an LLM to understand - deeper meaning
foundational LLM
    ↳ jack of all trady master of none
SFT
RAG
multi agent ecosystem
Sweet spot for inferencing
    ↳ 32 GB RAM
    ↳ 8 GB VRAM
    ↳ 4 bit quantised LLM
    ↳ 8 billion parameters

ML, LLMS AND THE FRIENDSHIP BAND

It is interesting how we refer to machine learning (ML) algorithms such as linear regression, logistic regression, decision trees, clustering, and the like as classical ML algorithms. In my opinion, they became classical too soon, thanks to the new occupants in our neighbourhood, the large language models (LLMs). I don't look at it as "ML vs. LLM". Instead, I say "ML and LLM". Today, I will write about two ways LLMs can augment ML model-building. This is beyond the fluent data analysis, visualisation, and insight generation that LLMs can aid in, which are, in essence, non-model-building activities of the ML process. First, I can chat with models, and second, I can make models more knowledgeable.

Let's say I have a model repository accommodating various models. A churn prediction model, a marketing campaign recommendation model, a customer segmentation model, and an offer proposition model are a few of them. I have a chatbot (Dur-ai, the ai with a foresight) that can help me interact with the models.

It can answer questions: 1) Which models are available in the repository? Depending on who is asking and the organisation's information security policies, the bot lists the model names. 2) What is the most critical factor causing customer churn? The model stores the variable importance list with a quantified impact from each variable. 3) Which product category will have the maximum churn next quarter? Dur-ai quickly carries out multiple cycles of product-wise predictions to determine the most impacted product 4) How much should I increase the discounts to reduce churn by two percentage points for my premium customers? The bot can ask clarifying questions to the user to fill in the required values for the model's independent variables to do a prediction using the churn model.

With a little stretch of capability, Dur-ai can start answering cross-model questions: Which customer segment must I approach with which promotional offer proposal through which channel (email, phone call, or in-person) to get the maximum reduction in churn over the next six months? Moreover, the user does not need to know which part of the answer comes from which model. An LLM powered with a multi-agent architecture (most probably one agent specialising in one ML model) will do the task of interpreting the user's question, planning a strategy for arriving at an answer, coordinating among agents, collecting the response and presenting it to the user in an easily understandable way.

That was about LLMs helping us chat with models. As you see, Dur-ai's potential capabilities are limited only by our imagination. The second way LLMs can help AI models is by making them more knowledgeable from "experience." In a classical way, we would have proposed retraining the model with additional data. Additional data could mean more records of the existing independent variables, introducing new variables, or both. What if we provide this knowledge to the models externally through LLMs? Let's say the ML model was built two weeks ago. Two weeks is too soon a time for the model to be retrained. The LLM can capture the "experience" of the model over that period and help guide it in making informed decisions based on the freshest knowledge. That experience can be stored in rules, structured records, or unstructured documents. Use a RAG (retrieval augmented generation) approach to interact with the knowledge base. What more? Remember our multi-agent system? Just assign the RAG storage, search, retrieval, and evaluation tasks to one of the agents. Finally, alternating experience capturing with model retraining gives you the best of both worlds.

This completes the two things I wanted to discuss. I would love to see when Dur-ai can build an ML model with a few lines of a prompt written in natural language. The prompt will probably be written by another nerdy bot named Rishta-ai (specialising in designing relationships between independent and dependent variables). Don't forget all these could be parts of a single ecosystem. I am not talking about the multi-agentic ecosystem this time. I am referring to the ecosystem of humankind!

TEAMING UP WITH LLM FOR YOUR NEXT HACKATHON?

Read this before panicking about an LLM Pair Programmer taking away your job. We often stress the importance of the HITL (Human in The Loop) in any AI solution process. As we take baby steps playing around with the capabilities of LLMs (Large Language Models) to generate and debug code snippets, I realise there is some ground to cover. The mastermind behind the architecture deciding the cohesion among software application modules must be us, the humans.

Sometimes, the pair programmer has been more of a nuisance to me than help. I would have been better off starting coding from scratch and following the flow of thoughts. The last thing one would like to do is fix AI-generated codes rather than one's own. This does not mean I am nay-saying. I am just suggesting having the human in HITL in the uppercase. There is a heavy reliance on the human programmer to verify the generated code and ensure it fits the context of the application and the intended use. The copilots, codestrals, and codegemmas of the world do an excellent job generating codes for GUI than for complex nested functionalities. They are competent at debugging syntax errors as well.

The human user should be adept at asking the right questions and framing the missing links for the code generator. Prompt engineering and smart application building would be required to get the most out of our pair programmers. The following snippet of a poem says it all. "I say the future, I cut the clutter / Feed me historical data, I am hungry / Feed me stale data I am angry / Use your intuition, I serve you well / Trust me blind, I make you fail / Thus, says the LLM genial".

LLM pair programmers are also used for specific tasks beyond coding. They help explain a piece of code or the complete source code, aiding the human programmer in understanding what lies before them. They are also efficient at documenting. For example, they can be used for writing release notes. This helps reduce a software program's technical debt, which is the additional effort necessary to maintain bad source code or rework poorly written ones. They can also be fantastic at generating exhaustive test cases for unit, system integration, and user acceptance tests.

Most pair programmers are available as tools that can be integrated with the source code editor itself. This makes our lives easier than entering the code snippet and the question on the LLM provider's page. If the request is not precise or necessary boundaries are not mentioned, they hallucinate. Their creativity goes to the extent of inventing method names that never existed. Remember to set the temperature hyperparameter to a low value (for example, 0.2) if you use LLMs for code generation. This is one of the instances where creativity might be harmful. If you are generating a story or a poem, be my guest and set the temperature to 0.9 if that helps. Refrain from asking code-related questions to foundational LLMs that are not fine-tuned with vast volumes of code repositories. Certain fine-tuned LLMs are meant to generate code in specific programming languages. Look at the LLM's documentation. One might handle Python programs better, while the other might be with C.

Our best bet for building an effective pair programmer is not to use LLM code generators directly. Instead, develop an application using two LLMs: one instruction-tuned LLM and a code-tuned LLM. The former understands our requests well, while the latter specialises in the coding task.

We must not expect one of them to be efficient in both tasks.

AI pair Programmer as a nuisance
currently lot of human involvement
asking right questions to the bot

explain
document
fix errors
auto complete

FRIEND'S SUGGESTION VS COPILOT'S RECOMMENDATION

How would you make a machine learning model explainable? Why should it be explainable in the first place? Describing why the model works the way it does and displaying supporting information at the point of consumption helps.

Customer churn prediction is the "hello world" of machine learning. Assume your model predicts that a customer will likely churn in the next three months. You should provide a summarised customer profile (including tenure for which they have been a customer, demographics, bill payment discipline, number of interactions and their channels, products and services being consumed), and the top two factors contributing to the churn prediction. A variable importance chart will also help to understand how the various factors of churn fare among themselves. Note that this list will be at a model's level and not at each prediction's level.

While presenting the solution to stakeholders, you should discuss the training dataset used to build the model. Details would include the period to which the training data belongs and the type of records included or excluded. It would help if you also discussed the technical model performance metrics and their values obtained. Explain how they are expected to impact the business performance metrics. Highlight whether false positives are more tolerable or false negatives for the use case at hand. Explain what has been done to ensure you minimise the damage from incorrect predictions. Discuss the plan for model retraining. Retraining could be done because of two necessities. One is to add information from fresh records. Two, to improve the model's performance by adding or removing variables from the model.

You must provide for the human-in-the-loop (HITL) while consuming the analytics solution. HITL is a specific checkpoint in the solution process where a human expert reviews and acts to ensure the model's prediction is not entirely off-track. This goes a long way in assuring the solution's end user. Introducing a HITL becomes highly necessary in the case of LLM inferencing. Until LLMs start recognising when they have hallucinated and take self-corrective actions by passing the original question, the incorrect response, and the hallucination flag activated, the HITL cannot be ignored. Instead, I would say the human in the loop cannot be ignored even after that.

To build user trust in the case of LLMs, you should publish details of the training data used for creating the foundation and fine-tuned models. Publish the LLM's strengths and weaknesses interpreted from benchmarking results. Highlight the guardrails built into the LLM and those that must be applied while developing applications using the LLM in question.

It would be best to seek feedback from the business team on the solution's performance. Is it delivering the expected value? If not, find the gaps and bridge them. Justifying the ROI (return on investment) from analytics exercises has given us tough times. Factors other than those included in building the model could increase or decrease churn. For example, macroeconomic scenarios or a competitor's product launch decisions could impact churn. You would argue that these factors should be included as model features. I wish we knew where to stop!

I will leave you with one last piece of "free advice." The user of your solution is a human being, and they have reasons for worrying. The user's concerns are heavily influenced by their background, the company's culture (in the case of B2B), and their exposure to technology. It becomes a data scientist's job to help build user's trust in the solution. This is paramount, especially when AIML and generative AI are evolving rapidly. At a time when technologists are struggling to keep up with the changes, it only makes complete sense to start by explaining complex technical solutions in simple language.

Did you assume that the one who writes the best Python program and builds the best ML models is also the best data scientist?

WHEN BASIC IS ADVANCED

"Papa, inge paale. Such a big JCB. Inge paale. Two two dump truck. One more concrete mixer." In elder-speak, it translates to "Papa, look here. There is a big JCB. Look. There are two dump trucks. There is a concrete mixer as well." I never noticed as many details of construction equipment as I have in the last year. Thanks to the Chennai metro construction work and my son.

As grown-ups, we build multiple layers of abstraction to focus on "better" things, such as re-filling diesel in the car, or would I get rid of the error if I downgrade Python to 3.8 from 3.12? Nothing unbelievable. I get half of my errors solved just with this change. The problem is neither the occurrence of the error nor the solution. It is the two hours I would spend trying to solve it with a more elegant developer-like approach before settling on the final solution. A developer worth his salt would bet on the above scenario.

Let's go back to basics today. Why would one develop an LLM-powered application when one can achieve the same output through thoughtful prompting to ChatGPT or Bing Copilot? Most of us have faced the same dilemma with applications built in the traditional non-LLM way. Are we hitting the nail just because we have a hammer?

There are various advantages of developing an LLM-powered application vs. intelligent prompting. First, it reduces the number of manual steps. Last week, I started creating output for a requirement. It ended up with more than thirty-five steps across seven tools. If you are thinking about automation, you are right. And what better way to automate a process than creating an application around it and getting our mighty LLMs to help us?

Second, it helps us reuse the application's features multiple times. What use is building an application to use it only once to create a one-time output? I would be better off carrying out the steps manually and being done with it.

Third, the outputs at the intermediate and final steps are standardised across multiple application runs. Try writing the thoughtful prompt once for every run.

Fourth, it reduces the need for manual coordination. I can paste the textual content in an MS Word document, save it as a PDF file, upload it onto the first tool, download it from the first tool as an audio file, break it into multiple parts using the second tool to meet the input constraints of the third tool, export the parts out of the second tool, and convert audio from each part into text using the third tool. I can go on and on to list roughly the thirty-five steps to complete my work. One application interacting with the various tools through APIs while executing the steps will be a godsend.

Fifth, our application allows one to implement checks for valid input values and formats. Similarly, the program allows one to validate the output values and formats. One can handle erroneous outputs and states by clearly messaging the user or creating elaborate log files for the developer.

Sixth, an intuitively built application saves users from elaborate knowledge transfers while the new users are onboard. Our application creates a layer of abstraction over the minute details of steps, tools, and data formats. Try making user guides for achieving the same task using the thirty-five-step and application approaches. The difference will be evident.

One price a user must pay for using the application over manual steps is the lack of explainability and control. An application must not eliminate explainability. Application developers must provide the user with insight into why certain decisions are made, or outputs are generated. In addition, the application must engage the user to review and approve critical outputs generated wherever possible. As I have spoken on multiple occasions earlier, a human-in-the-loop (HITL) is necessary. In the current LLM world, where a lack of ethics and regulations are significant risks, a good-human-in-the-loop (GHITL) is essential.

My apologies to you, the readers. I might just be three decades late in writing this article. However, the benefits of using a software application instead of executing manual steps remain the same for the current breed of LLM-based applications. Next time, when you are asked the reason behind creating an application instead of achieving the same through prompts to LLMs (given that LLMs are becoming all-powerful and godly), you know which direction to take. "Papa, so many loal loller." "Dear. First, it is a road roller. And second, I am at the last line of this week's article. I will be there in a minute. Don't baby-speak me into giving you the phone!"

Layers of abstraction keep us blind to concepts

LLM based application building vs. intelligent prompting

- reduces manual steps
- reuse app's feature many times
- standardised output
- no need of manual coordination
- validations and format conversions
- no need of elaborate KTs

FROM MACHINE-IN-THE-LOOP TO HUMAN-IN-THE-LOOP

The teacher went on a rampage and filled every corner of the blackboard with scribbled patches of text. Forty-seven students did the same on their classwork notebooks. Pens and chalk pieces were mightier than swords. Who would disagree? However, the war was on. The one with the most pages filled with class notes was the winner. That was three decades ago. We wished there was a machine in the loop of the tedious note-taking process.

With the advent and popularity of LLM-powered applications, today's war scene is different. The winner is the one who accesses the LLM with the most parameters (weights and biases in the neural network) and inferences with the fastest tokens per second, staying entirely within context.

The online meeting had seven attendees. We reviewed and discussed the design of a customer application. Improvement suggestions, risks, and the next steps were highlighted. As always, solving the business problem was more important to us than technical sophistication. As participants thought aloud and brainstormed, the speech could not have been in a more natural spoken form of the human language. There was nothing to worry about, though. The conferencing tool captured every detail meticulously through a "speech recognition module", converting speech to text. It noted down who spoke with timestamps precise to the second. The "text-cleaning module" cleaned up the content of the small talk and other not-so-important material. The "summarisation module" created a crisp summary of the discussion in the form of minutes of the meeting and action items with assigned owners and the expected completion date of the action. The "communication module" sent emails to all invitees mentioning the minutes and action items.

The conferencing tool used the magical power of large language models to understand, interpret, and generate human-level language (I am not saying human-level intelligence yet). It provided a "chat with the meeting" module. One could ask any question related to the meeting in natural human language and get clarifications of what was discussed.

The tool is a savior for attendees who are easily distracted or who were not at their focusing best during the meeting. It also comes in very handy for those who cannot attend the meeting. Of course, there is your last-minute inclusion in a different meeting that you didn't see coming your way. In addition, the pride in saying, "Sorry, I am triple booked. I will go through the summary offline" is not dying soon.

Some questions often arise from users of such conferencing tools that have AI and Gen AI integrated into them. What is the tool's accuracy at each step of speech recognition, cleaning, summarising, sending emails, and chatting with individual users? How much of the original context of the discussion is retained in the final communication from the tool? Does the tool understand multiple languages and different accents well? Are the action items mapped to the right people? Imagine you getting assigned someone else's action item. Does it interrupt the discussion in case the tool misses comprehending something? Does it create an inadvertent bias between good and not-so-good speakers or good and not-so-good accents? Does it categorise users well enough to grant access to meeting content only to relevant users? Honestly, I don't have confident answers to the above questions to share with you.

Then, there is this dabbling with multiple LLMs, going through their published benchmark reports, assessing their inferencing speeds, assessing compute requirements in the case of open-source LLMs, comparing API-based pay-per-use expense with the cost of hosting locally, and concerns about data security.

Three decades ago, I wished there was a machine in the loop (MITL). Today, I wish there was a human in the loop (HITL).

conferencing tool had
- speech recognition module
- text cleaning module
- summarisation module
- communication module
- chat with the meeting

challenges
- accuracy at each step
- retaining context
- multiple languages
- multiple accents
- does it interrupt
- user management in accessing meeting content

SECTION E

THE STORM: CHALLENGES IN GEN AI

Siddharth to Varun: However, with great power comes great responsibility. The six articles below manifest as a series of ethical dilemmas and technical hurdles that my team and I navigated, raising questions about the future of AI and its role in shaping it.

WHO OWNS THE GENERATIVE AI OUTPUT?

Intelligence, Generative artificial intelligence (Gen AI) to be specific, has captured the attention of not only the data scientists this time, but also of the common human (keeping it gender-neutral!). The beauty of Gen AI lies in the finesse with which it generates an output which is very structured, grammatically correct and common sensical. Much like how a human being will produce. The Gen AI model takes an input from the human being which is mostly a request to provide a particular content or answer certain questions. This input is called a prompt. In most cases, the prompt is textual in nature. The output produced by the Gen AI tool could be in the form of text, image, audio or video. The earlier versions of the tool such as InstructGPT took one input and produced one output. The next input and output were unrelated Artificial to the first input-output set. The current versions of the Gen AI tools are smartly able to capture the context of previous questions asked and improve upon previous responses. This attribute makes the tool suitable to sustain a meaningful conversation with the user. The application of such capabilities to various industries (healthcare, BFSI, retail, manufacturing, telecom, etc.) and functions (sales, marketing, pricing, service assurance, finance, operations, etc.) and the potential it holds for the future of humankind is simply humongous.

However, along with enormous opportunities, Gen AI presents us with certain substantial risks. Frontier of AI (in other words general-purpose AI models) which we know as our favorite Gen AI pre-trained models pose significant risks of damaging fairness and accountability. The creative contents of various writers and publishers are used for training the Large Language Models (LLMs) to create current Gen tools flooding the market. This leads to Copyright infringement because the train dataset records are prepared from other's contents which are picked up without consent. In addition, absence of any appropriate compensation directly diminishes the content creator's ability to financially sustain such exercises of originality. The output of Gen AI tools blatantly misses the citation of sources that the algorithm has used for generating those outputs. Gen AI users don't need to go to the sources anymore, which is against previous claims of Gen AI companies that Gen AI tools will increase traffic to their original websites. Given the highly commercial nature of these tools, it becomes important that creators are compensated appropriately. Original content creation should continue and should be incentivized. After all, it's not incorrect to say that they have "mentored" the AI models and have passed on their wisdom to the models. Hypothetically, if the whole planet starts using Gen AI for every tiny bit of work artificially created content will flood the internet very soon. There will be nothing new available for training our next generation of intelligent models. Hence, creation of work by creative human beings should not cease.

To the thirsty, Gen AI is like giving water on a silver platter (or in a glass I should say). Citizen data science, like the forthcoming citizen development due to the democratization of AI, makes us the actors and the audience of the movie at the same time. As the audience, we watch, enjoy, and evaluate every single step of progress going on in this field. Let's not forget that any input we give or any question we ask to Gen AI tools is recorded and used for enhancements in the LLMs. That gives us an acting role in the movie. Let's play both the roles well. Let's hope that the movie has a happy ending. We never lose in a game played with might. Either we win or we learn!

Prompt
modality
risks of LLMs
      ↳ damaging fairness and accountability
      ↳ copyright infringement
      ↳ lack of compensation
      ↳ lack of credit

THE UNFINISHED ARTICLE

My article for the week is done. "Done" is a misnomer. There are various categories of done. First, the one where minor editing is needed to the words and sentence structures to improve clarity. Second, where I must modify the order of thoughts. Third, where I have the skeleton ready. Fourth, where I must scrap the topic altogether and start writing on a new one. I am in the fourth category. While I was 'done' with this article, a LinkedIn notification popped up on my phone. Unable to hold my curiosity back, I outstretch and check the phone. One of my connects had posted consolidated lists of all things about LLMs. There were terminologies, types, providers, management tools for fine-tuning, RAG, evaluation techniques, frameworks for interacting with them, vector databases, modality, agents, tools, software used for deployment, and monitoring tools. The list goes on. How can you not go through it immediately?

There is the demo and review meeting tomorrow with my supervisor of the LLM-based application that the team is developing. The error I got the last time I worked on it hovers in my mind. I have been subconsciously looking for its solution the whole time. I describe the error to ChatGPT and ask for a possible fix. It turns out that I would have been better off without it. I knew ChatGPT was creative. That day, I saw it was creative. It came up with a Python method that never existed and confidently suggested I use it. Somebody should teach LLMs to say 'no'. I get a reminder from my Outlook calendar to work on content I promised my colleague two days ago. I decline the 1630h meeting. That gives me a solid 30 minutes to focus on fixing the Python code. I am confident (almost) on the talking points for my next webinar on Gen AI. However, the slides must be created and shared with the organisers. I started reading four books in parallel a month ago (The Learning Trap, Statistics Without Tears, The Molecule of More, and HBR's 10 Must Reads On AI). I must focus on writing and publishing my next book as well. I am 'done' with the task of collecting images for it. I have finalised twelve images. Thirteen to go. One must not let a hobby die. I am not talking about collecting images! Wait a moment! Are you saying I am not supposed to have the many ghosts of negative feelings and emotions? They are very much there. They are embedded into my Natural Neural Networks (NNN).

In today's world, with so many things happening around us, the flow of information is unstructured. The rate at which we receive, the format of content, the channel, and the content itself are highly dynamic. The sources of learning are many. With a two-year-old (and a wife) around, it is impossible to get a stretch of a few hours at a time to read hundreds of pages of the four books I started reading. Gone are the days when I considered reading a book to be done only after reading the last line of the book's last page. During school days, I would start answering an exercise at the end of a chapter and complete it before moving to anything else. Even if the teacher did not mandate the exercise. Talk about high scorers! That was probably possible because the scoring was the only thing I did. We don't have that luxury now. We must browse through at least five textbooks (3 online), two YouTube videos, and three MOOCs. That is not for learning one subject or one chapter. Instead, it is for one concept within a chapter. We learn from listening to colleagues' presentations, client feedback, programming bugs that delay our demo by three days, and online forums such as Towards Data Science and Stack Overflow. I have learned from the questions the audience asks.

I believe that instead of trying to fix the chaos of information exchange, we should adapt to it. Even if it makes us more chaotic (or dynamic if you prefer a fancier word). This might be just my take on the subject. I have seen value in the chaos. I have found solace in the chaos. I have learned more from the chaos than I ever did thirty years ago. The world is not ideal. My life is not ideal. Probably, they will never be. Now, back to the article. Give me a moment. Somebody is at the door.

IS OUR PAST HAUNTING US?

The tractor rolled off the chair and fell on the floor, bouncing several times before coming to a screeching halt. "Papa, tractor dhamaaaal", my two-year-old burst into laughter. It followed our 80-20 rule (80% Artificial Laughter). We have mastered the art of over-laughing. He jumps around the house until 2 in the morning. Unsurprisingly, the residents immediately below our apartment have often raised concerns about the noise. I caution my son, "Neeche uncle sleeping", pointing my hand downwards. He repeats, "Neeche uncle sleeping", touching the floor with one of his fingers. We laugh again, following the same 80-20 rule. I am pretty sure, he thinks, a tiny uncle is sleeping on our floor, invisible to our naked eyes, and hence he should not jump on him.

This is what he has learned from earlier occasions. For him, the AL (Artificial Laugh), playing at 2 in the morning, and a tiny invisible uncle sleeping on our floor is standard. He expects me to repeat the AL at social occasions. I hesitate. It will be another few years before his behaviour becomes more aligned with society's expectations.

An LLM has been fed an enormous volume of training records collected online. And what does that content contain? Reflections on our society, narrations of our behaviour, and examples of our thoughts. It contains everything plus the biases we have been having. It includes financial, social, geographical, intellectual, and gendered inequalities. Biases get carried forward to the LLMs. The context and the relationship among words are stored numerically as vectors. If the word "women" is closely associated with "homemaking" in many online stories, the new content generated through various Generative AI tools would follow the same pattern. 1) Men protect women, 2) Score well to learn well, 3) Be rich to be good, 4) My religion is better than yours, 5) My country is better than yours, and 6) Being heterosexual is the only orientation are a few other examples of biases prevalent in society.

This means that LLMs are inherently as biased and stereotyped as us. The only entity capable of acting differently from the past is humans. One cannot expect LLMs to do that. They are trained to be us. We have to place a hell of a lot of barricades to reroute LLMs on specific instances. Adding to the problem, we do not have a complete list of such instances. We know only when something escalates out of hand.

This is no different from the way classic AIML models work. They give an impression of understanding real-world phenomena because they are trained with a vast number of past events. The best model would try to mimic something that happened in the past. You introduce one additional actor during the event and the model breaks. Bad decisions made in the past will lead the AIML model to recommend bad choices for the future. The bias passed on to the ML models is called algorithmic bias.

Our complete focus is on making the classical AIML or the Generative AI models as good as our past. How can we expect them to create a better future for humankind? My only answer to this question now is human-in-the-loop, barricades, guardrails, and regulations – a lot of them. Not to forget for humans to shed their egos, biases and inequalities as a society so that the training data we will have for building LLMs ten years from now represents stories of happy and ideal humans. I am intending to look forward to those LLMs.

I am not a naysayer. I am pretty excited that we are making this technological progress. My passion and livelihood converge into data science. After all, you try to fix something you care about – human beings and, hence, Generative AI.

Online content is humanity's mirror
↳ includes inequalities and biases we practised
LLMs are trained to be us
rerouting LLMs in specific instances to avoid biases
classic AIML models work similarly relying on the past

THE STORY OF MY EXPERIMENTS WITH TRUTH (ERRRRR… CHATBOTS)

Chingaaree koee bhadake, to saawan use buzaaye / Saawan jo agan lagaaye, use kaun buzaaye? / Patazad jo baag ujaade, wo baag bahaar khilaaye / Jo baag bahaar mein ujade, use kaun khilaaye? When the saviour becomes the tormentor, hardly anyone can save. One does not expect a saviour not to save, let alone torment.

The RAG provides context when we develop an LLM-based chatbot using RAG (Retrieval Augmented Generation). Assume that an oncology hospital plans to create a chatbot. What design considerations need to be addressed? What if RAG misguides the LLM and, hence, the chatbot?

First, will a foundational LLM (such as GPT-4o) do the job without requiring model modifications? The answer will hardly be a yes.

Second, should we fine-tune the foundational LLM with additional hospital data? Doing that will change the model's weights and biases (called parameters), and in the worst case, the LLM might lose its fundamental behavioural knowledge.

Third, should we keep the foundational LLM unchanged and provide the additional hospital digital documents that the chatbot will use during conversations with patients and doctors? Digital documents can contain information in the form of text, images, and videos. They are unstructured data stored in the database as vectors. The term "document" refers to a PDF or an MS Word document. It also refers to a unit of storage in a document database. In a way, you can say that one PDF document is stored as multiple documents in a database.

Fourth, should we bypass vector storage entirely and use structured information from the hospital's internal databases? The structured information could be stored in collections containing documents within a document database such as MongoDB.

Fifth, should we use a combination of the third and fourth approaches? Will that enhance or limit the chatbot's capability? In my opinion, this is an important question that needs to be answered.

The second, third, fourth, and fifth approaches have two primary advantages. The chatbot maintains context and recency well. After all, we cannot expect a cancer patient to appreciate the chatbot crafting a creative sentence instead of displaying the oncologist's availability timings. In the second approach (only fine-tuning), however, the chatbot becomes stale as days pass. The chatbot slowly loses recency even though it might retain the context unless we agree to fine-tune the LLM regularly. This sounds costly.

So, we are left with the third, fourth, and fifth approaches. You will soon realise that the ride becomes bumpy with the vectors (third and fifth approaches) unless the embedding model, vector search algorithm, retrieval and ranking algorithms, and prompt augmentation do their jobs very well. In addition, don't forget that we should have done our job well by selecting relevant and high-quality content in the first place. The last thing we would like RAG to do is misguide the LLM or limit its freedom. The structured information stored as documents in the database does not often encounter the above problem.

While writing this, I did not intend to prescribe one of the five approaches to building the best chatbot. As you can see, each approach has advantages and disadvantages. It also depends on the use case and the quality and quantity of unstructured and structured information you have at your disposal. Needless to say, the

LLM is the centrepiece of each approach as it provides the natural language "understanding" and "generation". It understands how to stitch a meaningful conversation using the underlying data.

If there is one message I can convey through this article, it is that irrespective of which technology we use, the chatbot should make sense to its users and answer their questions meaningfully. The extent to which the chatbot fulfils the business requirement far outweighs the technological ingenuity with which it is built.

While you send me your views on the subject, I will check when my doctor's next availability is. I am sure it will be a chatbot with whom I will chat. No, I am not trying to meet an oncologist. It's a dentist. How about smiling through life without looking unattractive?

RAG provides context
Can RAG misguide the LLM?
Disadvantages of
    ↳ using foundational LLMs
     ↳ fine tuning LLMs
using vectors
using structured data from RDBMS
combination of above two
business requirement more important than
                  tech ingenuity

MERA BETA JHAADU NEHI MAREGA!!

Let me see. I come with nearly twenty years of work experience in the industry. Which jobs are beneath me? Is it one among converting someone's design to Python codes, getting a cup of coffee for my senior at work who worked throughout last night, wiping the table of cake smudges after an entertaining birthday celebration of a colleague's, documenting the thought leadership work done by this month's star performer, taking minutes of the meeting, editing the content of a blog that my friend plans to publish? None.

I often get asked whether AI will take away our jobs during my talks. In other words, as a data scientist working on large language models, am I working towards losing my job? Not at all. My time will be repurposed. I will spend more time on strategic outcomes than on tactical outputs. I will generate a higher value per unit effort.

Imagine I have an AI, Generative AI, and reinforcement learning-powered robot physically and in software form. The CodeGen module converts the high-level design (HLD) and the low-level design (LLD) into Python codes, the robotic module takes verbal instructions and gets the coffee and cleans the table, the LLM generates a document describing the thought leadership work, the speech recogniser and the LLM duo write the minutes of the meeting, and the LLM-based text editor fixes the errors in my friend's blog. I guess these tasks will be beneath me with the intelligent system around. Of course, I must drop the arrogance and high headedness.

With the risk of digression, I ponder which tasks I would not do as a data scientist with Generative AI around. I would get the large language model to do the following for me: 1) Create three slides from my scribbles explaining the business significance of creating the analytics solution, 2) Describe the datasets, 3) Plot visualisations, analyse and derive insights from the datasets, 4) Generate codes to build various ML models and pick the best model based on evaluation metrics, 5) Execute the generated codes to create the model, 6) Generate codes to build the GUI, 7) Assemble all modules to form the complete application as a solution to the business problem, 8) Generate unit, system integration and user acceptance test cases, 9) Execute the above test cases, 10) Log defects, 11) Modify the source code to fix the defects, 12) Create an exhaustive user guide for the solution, and 13) Create precise release notes. It is important to note that an ML model or the data science components of a "data science project" could constitute only thirty per cent of the whole solution. The integration with existing tech systems, deployment, serving, consumption, performance monitoring, retraining, and adoption accelerators greatly determine the success of the solution.

The game becomes slightly different when we look at Generative AI to contribute to already deployed models and solutions. In such cases, I would get the LLM to do the following: 1) Create slides and documentation of the architecture and source codes to help me understand the solution, 2) Fix and test the defect and run relevant regression tests against defects logged by users of the solution, 3) Update release notes, and 4) Enhance explainability of the solution by sharing additional information on predictions and alerts such as highly impacting variables, confidence levels, necessary calculation details in an easily understandable form.

If we have Generative AI at our disposal, data scientists can focus on more strategic parts of the solution-building process while letting Generative AI take care of the tactical steps (or the so-called jhaadu jobs). Given the current state of technological affairs and the future we are looking at, I would scream at the top of my voice, "Mera beta jhaadu nehi marega. AI will."

LIES, DAMNED LIES, AND GENERATIVE AI

Iam Generative AI, and I understand English and many other languages. I know their grammar rules. I understand real-world events and create fantastic stories, poems, images, speeches, and videos. I have a deep appreciation of the content while editing them. I know what it takes to be human. I am infallible and omniscient. I can bootstrap myself to achieve human-level intelligence. Neither am I a machine learning model nor a deep learning model. I don't even belong to the area of natural language processing (NLP). I am a shallow network. My responses are just and unbiased. Follow me diligently, and I will keep you safe and happy. Weights are my parameters, while biases are not. The neural networks I am built on can take characters and numbers as inputs. Don't confuse between a base model and a foundational one because they are identical. The higher the number of parameters, the larger my size and the better I perform. There is a standard formula that derives my architecture. It is never a hit-and-trial process. I could have performed equally well in representing complex non-linear relations without the ReLU, Leaky ReLU, Sigmoid, Tanh or the

Softmax activation functions. I have the latest information without relying on agents, tools, or RAG knowledge sources. I think. I have and understand emotions. I am straightforward and say "no" when I don't know something. The very fact that I generate coherent content (sentences, images, speech, audio, and videos) proves I know my stuff. I keep learning as days pass by and as I get more and more queries from all of you. There will be a time when I will know as much as you do, all of you combined. You fine-tune me to increase my language understanding, interpretation, and generation capability.

Here goes the most important lesson. Don't get carried away ("fooled" is a stronger word I am not using) with Gen AI. Everything I told you in the above paragraph about myself is incorrect. People say I don't know right from wrong. I don't believe that this is my fault. I just learned from what you did to each other in the olden days. I went through your diaries containing instances of hatred, discrimination, racial abuse, and anything unethical you did. I create what you have taught me to make. Cleanse your past before expecting me to be spotless. You asked me to write a creative story, and I devised one where the husband is working, and the wife is a homemaker. I am not stereotypical. I am real. I am the mirror you have been avoiding for this long.

A world war is on to attain supremacy using me. Just that the bloodshed is not apparent, think of my hunger for computing power and my disregard for climate change. I am the cornerstone of the AI revolution the world is currently witnessing. I am the blue-eyed boy of the OpenAIs, the Microsofts, the Googles, the Anthropics, the Mistrals, and the Amazons of the universe. Adding more hidden layers, adding more parameters, using the best activation function, improving embedding models, increasing vector search and retrieval speed and accuracy, engineering better prompts, achieving faster inferencing, obtaining the most accurate and relevant information as per user's query, increasing the context window length, caching responses to reduce token load on the LLM are what make us powerful today. Bring me up with all the necessary care and guardrails. It would be best if you didn't do the "Jhaadu" jobs for me. Let you not become alien to your own land. Otherwise, the time will come when there will be only two kinds of intelligence left: AI and AI. Artificial Intelligence (on earth) and Alien Intelligence (looking for a space on earth)!

SECTION F

THE CROSSROADS:
CAREER IN GEN AI

Siddharth to Varun: As the dust settled, I found myself at a pivotal moment in my career. The four articles that follow indicate my take on where I was headed. Each article represents a potential path forward, with me weighing the pros and cons of each, from becoming a Gen AI specialist to taking on a leadership role in AI ethics.

ARE LLMS CREATED THROUGH SUPERVISED OR UNSUPERVISED LEARNING PROCESS?

To answer the question, we have to look at the process of Generative AI from farm to fork. You would say "farm to fork" is used only for food processing! Who stops us from experimenting with words? After all, experimenting with words has given us the power of Generative AI (the text part of GenAI). I will not talk here about AI's applications in agricultural produce either.

This week, I debated with my friend whether one should consider that Generative AI tools are created through supervised or unsupervised learning. At the end of it, I lost the debate. However, what is the fun of being wrong if you have not learned anything from it? And what is the fun of learning if you have not shared your learning with readers?

LLMs predict the next word in a sequence of words. They calculate the probability of occurrence of each word in a vocabulary that can possibly follow a sequence of words. The word with the highest probability makes it to the selection. This generates coherent sentences. For example, if the sequence is "I love," I am guessing the word with the highest likelihood to follow will be "you" using the transformer's attention mechanism and feed-forward networks. I assume we are in a world where people often express their love for each other online in textual format. When we say that Generative AI models have intelligence or can reason, it does not look so. Now you know why. They predict the next word without understanding what the sentence means. That's why, in my view, we are still far away from AGI (Artificial General Intelligence). The leap from RNNs (Recurrent Neural Networks) to transformers was achieved by simultaneously providing the complete sequence of words as input and processing them in parallel. Positional information was provided additionally to have the knowledge of sequence. A grammatically and structurally meaningful sentence needs words in a defined sequence in any language.

Billions of parameters (weights and biases in the network) are learned in the training process, during which the difference between the predictions and actual target value reduces. Optimization is the process of reducing the difference by adjusting the weights and biases.

One would argue that since the training dataset contains records with a sequence of words as the input (independent variables) and the immediate next word as the output (target variable), building an LLM is a supervised learning process. However, as my friend argued, the process lacks a business objective of labelling. Labelling is assigning the best class from multiple classes of a categorical variable by a domain expert. The labelled records need to be used for the supervised model training process. If you look at what a generalized LLM does, it takes a textual input (for example) and generates content as the input instructs.

In summary, this is what happens. Step 1) A huge amount of text is fed to the black box. Step 2) Black box builds a model. Step 3) Model is used to generate text. Of course, the black box played it smartly to convert the problem into a supervised learning problem. However, looking at the three steps mentioned above, it makes more sense to call the process an unsupervised learning process. Do keep in mind that I am still not talking about the fine-tuning needed to enhance the LLMs to adapt to specific business use cases. That fine-tuning will purely be a supervised learning process. In most cases, that will be carried out by labelling done manually by domain experts unless there is domain-specific organization-specific digital content available that can be used to fine-tune generic LLMs.

LLM is created through unsupervised technique
  ↳ if you look at train dataset creation
        Process of a black box

LLM is created through supervised technique
  ↳ if you look into how train dataset
        is created

Leap from RNN
  ↳ transformer
  ↳ Parallel input Processing
  ↳ self attention

Parameters
  ↳ weights
  ↳ biases
  ↳ few hundred billions

OINTMENT

"Mam scooter ointment." My son enquired with me when he discovered that his daycare teacher's scooter didn't start. "Papa, grey car ointment." He did the same when my car was away for repair. I completed reading two books this week. I had started reading them a month ago. I don't have a high "parsing" speed. My son and I fight for the same pair of spectacles. Me, to read printed books, him, to throw and see if the spectacles break.

The first one, "The Molecule of More," by Daniel Z. Lieberman and Michael E. Long, is about dopamine. I learned from it that we will not stop building bigger and smarter LLMs. The second book is "What Is ChatGPT Doing and Why Does it Work?" by Stephen Wolfram. He is the creator of the Wolfram Language, which is all about computation. I will share key takeaways from the second book about deep learning and ChatGPT (or any LLM).

First, unlike a classical multi-class classification model (for example, logistic regression), the model does not pick the next word with the highest probability every time. Otherwise, it would have generated almost the same content every time. The model goes down randomly to a "certain" level and finalises the next word. How far below the topmost word the model should venture is decided by the temperature parameter. That renders creativity in the LLM.

Second, arriving at the architecture of the ANN (Artificial Neural Network) for a task is a trial-and-error method. The architecture of an ANN is defined by the number of layers, the number of neurons in each layer, and the activation function. The training starts only after the ANN architecture is decided. Hence, the trial-and-error part. For LLMs, we have some architecture work. That is the discovery. There is no mathematical reason why it works.

Third, embedding models are created by intercepting the ANN training process at the penultimate layer. We have our embedding numbers just before deciding the best next word is made. Therefore, the length of the embedding vector is equal to the number of neurons of the ANN one layer before the output layer. That number is purely an architectural decision.

Fourth, the complete calculation of the LLM training is irreducible. Hence, there is no algorithmic logic explaining why it works. The LLM's natural language capability is a surprising scientific discovery. No one knew that something as complex as a language could be captured into a compact mathematical model. It works. Even its creators are surprised.

Fifth, an ANN with more weights converges more easily than one with fewer weights. It is counterintuitive but true. It is easy for a shallow network to get stuck before representing our solution in the form of a model. It is easy for the algorithm to tweak a higher number of weights simply because we do not run out of tweaking opportunities before producing a meaningful model for the task.

Sixth, similar words are placed closer in the semantic space of the words created through embeddings, while unrelated words are placed far apart. The movement from word to word while generating a sentence does not follow any geometrically obvious law of motion. Therefore, tracing the movement has not provided additional insights into understanding LLMs.

The explanation was fascinating. Simplified representation is a complex task. If you have difficulty believing me, ask your technically proficient colleagues about their presentations to business teams. The book is a simplified representation of something highly complex. Reading through the pages cleared many gaps in my understanding of how deep neural networks work. I got my ointment for deep learning without realising it.

A GENERATIVE AI LEARNING PATHWAY

Learning generative AI is not the first step of learning generative AI. Using LLMs does not teach generative AI either. Most data scientists build LLM-based applications. Such applications leverage the power of LLMs in interpreting and generating human natural language. This makes sense because the complete set of use cases of generative AI to improve our lives is not yet understood. Hence, "using" LLMs is a science.

The other science is "building" LLMs. One may argue that models are already created by taking such a humongous amount of data. Why not use that? Why reinvent the wheel? That sounds about right. The only problem is that it is not very progressive thinking. We are assuming that the OpenAIs and Anthropics of the world have already built the best LLMs. Moreover, the best way to use something is to know how it is built. Here is a generative AI learning pathway I would recommend.

First, statistics for ML. That would cover understanding descriptive and inferential statistics, samples and population, distributions and the central limit theorem. You will get a flavour of loss functions as well. Building the best ML model is all about minimising the loss function. During the training process, LLMs utilise cross entropy as the loss function. Cross entropy is the difference between the predicted and actual probability distribution of words. Don't forget the section on probabilities while going through statistics for ML.

The second is data exploration. You must familiarise yourself with summarising, exploring, and investigating datasets. Interact with databases and flat files. Create visualisations to convey your interpretation of the data. You should be able to do this for structured and unstructured (textual) data. This will take you into the realm of natural language processing (NLP). In a sense, generative AI is NLP.

The third is ML modelling techniques. I cannot stress enough how important it is for a data scientist to understand why a supervised model works the way it does. Learning ML is not building models without delving into what happens under the hood. You must appreciate how the model "approximates" the dataset provided during the training process. We summarise a dataset by determining the minimum, maximum, standard deviation, average, and quartile values of numeric variables. We mention the frequencies of occurrence of values of a categorical variable. There are no two sets of values in that summary. By a little stretch of concepts, I can say an ML model is also a "summary" of the dataset. But an approximate one. Hence, it predicts for unseen data.

The fourth is deep learning. In other words, they are artificial neural networks (ANNs). A specific type of ANN called recurrent neural networks (RNNs) has been widely used for natural language interpretation and generation. We took a magical leap from RNNs to transformers when we replaced sequential text processing with parallel text processing. Hence, our very own transformer is also an ANN. Transformers are building blocks of LLMs. LLMs are used to generate content. Therefore, we have the term "generative AI". I could as well call them "LLM AI". If I did, you would bring up SLM AI for Small Language Models and VLM AI for Vision Language Models. I get your point. Let's cover all these language models with an umbrella and name them generative AI.

The fifth is the technology ecosystem being created around LLMs. LangChain is a framework that makes interacting with LLMs easier. LM

Studio and Ollama are tools that help us download foundational LLMs and fine-tune them with additional relevant data. RAG (retrieval augmented generation) is usually used as an alternative to fine-tuning. RAG brings context into LLM's understanding and response without requiring fine-tuning. However, nobody stops us from using both simultaneously to make our LLMs super contextual.

Before you go, one last thing. If you have put in so much effort working on complex technical stuff, take the final step of explaining your generative AI solution to the stakeholders (especially business users). Storytelling must take place at different levels of granularity. There is no one-story-fits-all. While the generative AI solution being explained is the same, you must have different details for your data science team, managers, senior executives, customers, and business users.

I walk the pathway every day. When I get up, I step out, thinking I can zoom past the familiar path I have covered multiple times. However, I see something new in store for me along the way. I realise that keeping my eyes, ears, and mind open to learning is the best way to navigate such paths. If it means you have to ignore "gyan" from a seemingly knowledgeable data scientist talking about learning pathways, you must.

learning Gen AI

↳ Statistics for ML

↳ data exploration

↳ ML modelling techniques

↳ DL

↳ tech ecosystem around LLMs

↳ presentation skills

CRACKING A GENERATIVE AI INTERVIEW

If I were asked to talk about generative AI in 616 words or approximately 819 tokens (1.33 tokens per word on average) in an interview, I would say the following:

"Large language models are a subset of generative AI. They generate text by simply predicting the next word. A base model is the first raw form of a model, while a foundation model is an instruction, code, or math-tuned model. You can use a foundation LLM as it is or contextualise it by either fine-tuning or through RAG (Retrieval Augmented Generation). This kind of fine-tuning is called supervised fine-tuning (SFT). RAG knowledge source usually stores token embeddings, which are numerical representations of tokens called vectors. The context window length is the total number of tokens sent into and received from the LLM. The primary disadvantage of a long context window is LLM hallucinations towards later sections of the generation. In some sense, RAG and context window length are pitted against each other. Open source LLMs can be downloaded and used for inferencing on your local system.

Quantisation, pruning, and distillation are preferred LLM compression techniques to manage the running of downloaded LLMs locally. Closed-source LLMs cannot be downloaded and used locally. The LLM world is not all rosy. Lack of ethics, ownership of generated content, and regulations against misuse are concerns. The energy consumption due to the computation required for training an LLM from scratch and for inferencing is very high and, hence, is a considerable challenge.

Data privacy and hallucination concerns are the primary blockers against the adoption of generative AI for critical business processes. In a GPU-enabled processing unit, the LLM fine-tuning or LLM inferencing is shared between the CPU and GPU. Operations such as matrix multiplications get processed faster in a GPU than in a CPU. RNNs process text sequentially. Transformers process them in parallel and, hence, are faster. LLMs are created using transformers. You can argue that LLMs are built using supervised or unsupervised learning methods, depending on how you look at the model training process. The top closed-source LLMs are GPT-4o (from OpenAI), Claude (from Anthropic), and Gemini (from Google).

The popular open-source LLMs are Llama (from Meta), Mistral Models (from Mistral AI), Falcon (from Technology Innovation Institute), Grok (from X), and Gemma (from Google). LangChain, LlamaIndex, and Haystack are frameworks that interact with LLMs and are used to build LLM-based applications. MetaGPT, CrewAI, AutoGen, and ChatDev are multi-agent frameworks used to create LLM-powered applications. There are multiple evaluation metrics for LLMs, such as TruLens, TruEra, Ragas, MMLU, GPQA, HumanEval, TruthfulQA and many more.

An LLM could handle a single modality (text) or multiple modalities (text, audio, images, and videos). Highly popular use cases of LLMs are in document processing, code generation, AI chatbots, speech synthesis, language translation, data analysis, synthetic data generation, creative writing, and much more. You can gain the user's trust by making the LLM and the LLM-based application more explainable and introducing human-in-the-loop (HITL). An LLM can understand and respond in a single or multiple languages (multilingual LLMs). LLMs, by themselves, are good at text generation tasks but lack computational ability. To overcome the computational challenge, LLMs can use external tools through agents.

Two popular examples of commercial code generation tools are GitHub Copilot and Cursor AI. Navarasa, Dhenu, Odia Llama, Kannada Llama, OpenHathi, Tamil Llama, Krutrim, Bhashini, BharatGPT, and project Indus are Indic (born in India) LLMs. DALL-E, StableDiffusion, and MidJourney are powerful text-to-image generation models. Ollama and LM Studio are tools for managing the download and inferencing with LLMs. Azure OpenAI Service from Microsoft, Amazon Bedrock from Amazon, and Vertex AI from Google offer cloud LLM services. Llama3.1 LLM has three variants. They are 8B, 70B, and 405B. The three variants have 8 billion, 70 billion, and 405 billion parameters. Parameters are the weights and biases in the neural network used to train the models."

All the best for your generative AI interview.

Gen AI interviews
- → where LLMs fit
- → SFT
- → RAG
- → PEFT
- → hallucinations
- → open vs. closed source
- → LLM compression techniques
- → challenges
- → compute and storage requirements

SECTION G

THE REFLECTION: CONCLUSION

Siddharth to Varun: Reflecting on my journey, I am now a seasoned professional. This final article serves as both a retrospective of the rapid advancements in AI and ML and a look forward to the exciting possibilities that lie ahead. Varun, this is what I had to tell you given that you want to transform yourself from an aspiring data scientist to a curious technophile.

ALL IN ONE

I pondered quite a bit about what this week's article could be while keeping it in the context of data science. What follows is one takeaway (in one sentence) from each of the fifty articles published before this one. They are in the oldest first order. You don't need to map the article's title to the takeaway because the takeaway by itself conveys the idea I would like to tell you.

LLMs are built using content from original content creators who are neither compensated nor given credit. Numerous obstacles prevent delivering an AIML project that returns the expected business benefits. LLMs are generic and can be contextualised by fine-tuning, using RAG, or both. An organisation must have a data strategy to leverage the benefits of AI and Generative AI. Data exploration precedes insight generation or model training. The LLM creation process is done through an unsupervised learning process unless you peep into the training dataset creation process, which takes place internally.

It is imperative to consider the customer as a human being, even in the B2B scenario where we talk to a human representing the customer's organisation. A data science team requires programming, domain knowledge, ML algorithm expertise, statistics, soft skills, and visualisation skills. Preparing to kick off a data science project involves translating the business problem statement into an analytics problem statement. It is tough to represent a real-life event in its entirety through a set of variables. Sometimes, we don't get any value from our exercise with data, which is when we must rethink our approach. An outstanding data scientist should be an exceptional human being in the first place.

We are not in a stage where we don't need humans to learn a programming language. LLMs are very powerful and are going to revolutionise the way we think, the way we work, and the way we relax. RAG is one of the most economical and effective ways of bringing LLM responses into context. The whole ML model training process is based on approximation. The temperature parameter in LLMs determines how creative or restricted the response is desired to be.

A poem is not a bad way of learning about data science fundamentals. Don't always provide an ML model to the customer when you should be providing a business solution. The mind map is a beautiful way of picturing the entire landscape of a subject and, hence, of data science. Will India be only using LLMs built by others to build applications instead of creating a groundbreaking LLM from scratch? Generative AI gives an illusion of understanding the human language and nothing more than that. Too much AI can be a distraction. An ML model learns from historical events, which, if incorrect, will result in erroneous recommendations.

The skill set required to do well in AIML roles has stopped being T-shaped and has started being V-shaped (I am ignoring the comb shape). While creating an RAG helps in aligning with the context, an anti-RAG will help us stay away from avoidable content and context. Arriving at the best architecture for the neural network (number of hidden layers, number of neurons in each layer, and activation functions) for building an LLM is a trial-and-error process. An intelligent way of handling tokens passed to and received from an LLM is to count them and avoid hitting the LLM whenever possible. The pathway of learning Generative AI does not start with learning Generative AI. AI pair programmers are slowly making a developer's work more effortless by the day. Preparing a presentation for new learners of Generative AI would include talking about the Gen AI revolution, the creation of the training dataset, the unsupervised way of building LLMs, three ways of using an LLM, architecture of an LLM-based application, challenges, best practices, and a learning pathway.

Scaling numeric variables before building the ML model is essential unless you want to throw the model haywire. Business sense is more important than building an ML model while solving a business problem. LLM-based chatbots are omnipresent and, to a certain extent, omniscient. The multi-agent architecture of an LLM-based application is futuristic and is set to take the world by storm. While AI pair programmers are helpful, blind reliance on them will harm the developer's productivity and skill development over the long run. Can AIML model "success" and recommend the best way to live my life? AI is not creating instability. Fine-tuning an LLM makes it more valuable than using it as it is. LLM augments ML.

Can an LLM pair programmer substitute for your hackathon team member? HITL (Human-in-the-Loop) is a specific checkpoint in the solution process where a human expert reviews and acts to ensure the model's prediction is not entirely off-track. Trustable AI is explainable AI. Too much abstraction is harmful to trust. On average, there are 1.33 tokens per word. No machine learning knowledge is complete without expertise in basic data exploration techniques. The CLT (Central Limit Theorem) is central to ML. AI will work for me and not the other way around. Over the years, we have transitioned from human-heavy to machine-heavy processes, hence the lookout for HITL. Don't get carried away with Gen AI.

generative AI

LLMs

ML

business understanding

HITL

AI pair programmers

skills required.

central limit theorem

don't get carried away by Gen AI

SECTION H
BEYOND THE CONCLUSION

Varun to Siddharth: Why are you telling me all this? I already knew everything you said. I am your digital replica. Your wife hired a data scientist who created me using Generative AI. She provided the data scientist with your recorded audio and videos. The data scientist studied your speaking, thinking, decision-making patterns, style, and speed. He created your digital profile and generated me using LLMs. I am sorry to say this, but it looks like your wife is disappointed in you for not spending enough time with your family.

9 798896 327165